WORLD DATA ARTBOOK

Bernd Riemann

Copyright © 2019 Bernd Riemann

ISBN: 9781696915076

*For
Hatuey José Cabrera Pérez*

TABLE OF CONTENTS

SOCIETY

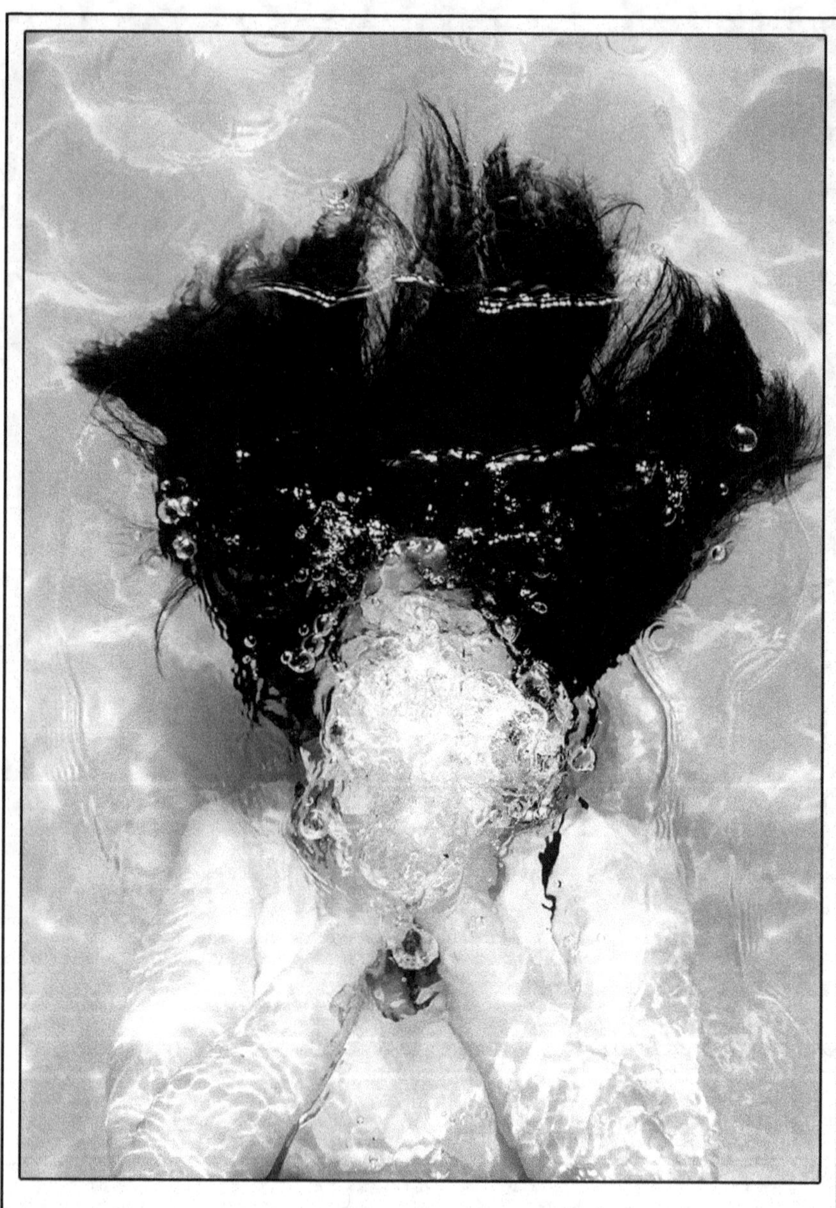

70% of human behavior is based on emotions, not reason
Source: GALLUP
Photo: Guilherme Yagui

Serious threats to civic freedoms
exist in more than 100 countries
Source: Oxfam International
Photo: Willy AuYeung

Only 4% of the world's population live in countries
where governments are properly respecting
the freedoms of association, peaceful assembly and expression
Source: CIVICUS
Photo: Alisdare Hickson

1 in 6 children live in areas of the world
affected by war or armed conflict
Source: United Nations
Photo: AMISOM Public Information

The annual United Nations Peacekeeping budget
is less than 0.5% of global military spending
Source: United Nations
Photo: Fabien Rafowicz

Since 1946, more than 170 cases have been entered
in the General List of the International Court of Justice
Source: United Nations
Photo: MIchael Coghlan

The Universal Declaration of Human Rights
is the most translated work in the world
Source: United Nations
Photo: University of Essex

Men own 50% more of the world's wealth than women,
and control over 86% of corporations
Source: Oxfam International
Photo: August Brill

Well over 11 million people are held in penal institutions
throughout the world
Source: Institute for Criminal Policy Research
Photo: Young Shanahan

Males account for 93% of the total prison population
Source: Institute for Criminal Policy Research
Photo: Allen Warren

More than 450,000 people across the world
are victims of homicidal violence every year
Source: UNODC
Photo: Tex Texin

Half of world's teens experience
peer violence in and around school
Source: UNICEF
Photo: Erika Mayumi Ozassa

3 in 10 students in 39 industrialised countries
admit to bullying peers
Source: UNICEF
Photo: Coastal Elite

Around 15 million adolescent girls aged 15 to 19
have experienced forced sex in their lifetime
Source: UNICEF
Photo: Sodanie Chea

35% of women worldwide have experienced
either physical and/or sexual intimate partner violence
or non-partner sexual violence in their lifetime
Source: World Health Organization
Photo: Saws

200 million women and girls have undergone
female genital mutilation
Source: Oxfam International
Photo: Tiomax80

Approximately 650 million girls and women
alive today were married before their 18th birthday
Source: UNICEF
Photo: mrhayata

Globally, women are accorded only
3/4 of the legal rights that men enjoy
Source: World Bank
Photo: AMISOM Public Information

At current rates of change, it will take 217 years to close the gap
in pay and employment opportunities between women and men
Source: Oxfam International
Photo: Ralf Steinberger

Women comprised 39% of the workforce in 2018,
but held only 27% of managerial positions
Source: United Nations, The Sustainable Development Goals Report 2019
Photo: Zyan

In 2018, young women were more than twice as likely
as young men to be unemployed or outside the labour force
and not in school or in a training program
Source: United Nations Statistics Division
Photo: Bread for the World

In nearly all OECD member countries,
the majority of university graduates are women
Source: Yale University
Photo: Alan Light

On average, women spend roughly triple the amount of time
that men do each day in unpaid care and domestic work
Source:: ,United Nations Statistics Division (UNSD)
Photo: mrhayata

750 million adults still remain illiterate
Source: United Nations
Photo: Ryan Hadley

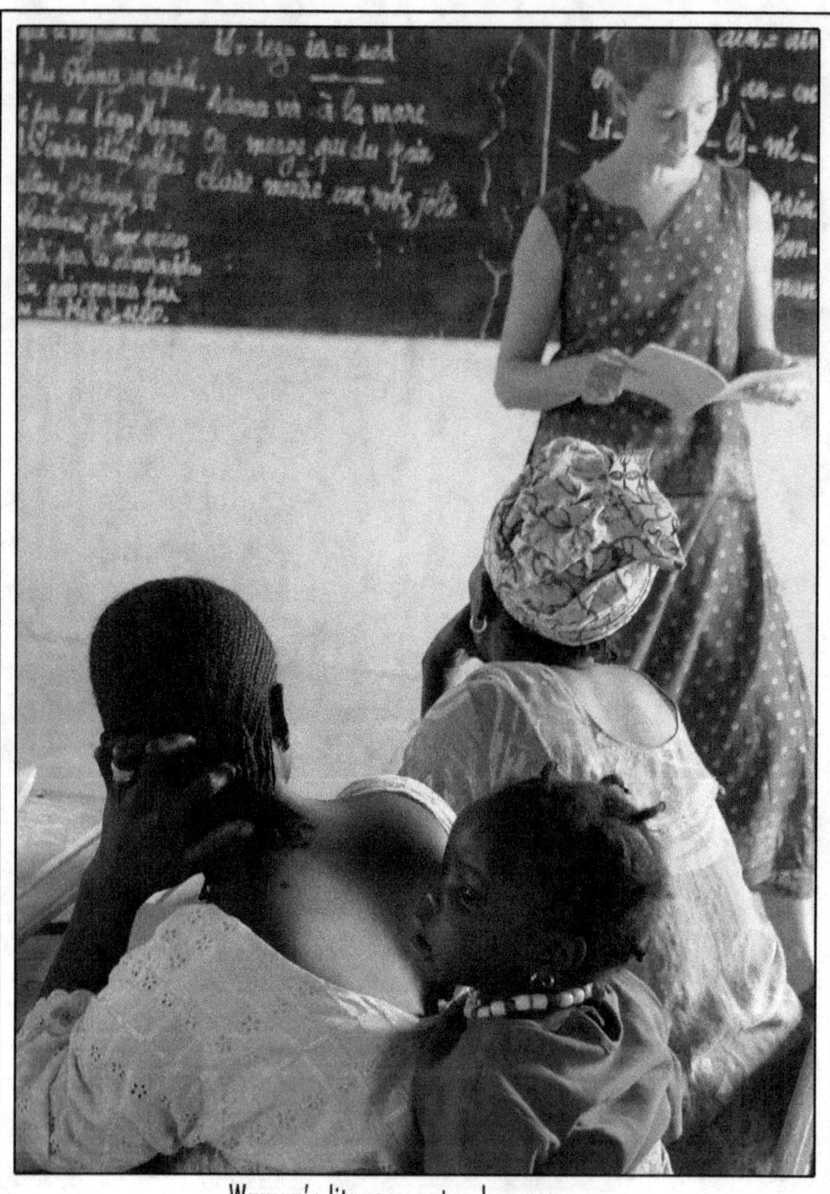

Women's literacy rates have grown
faster than men's literacy rates
in all regions over the past 25 years
Source: United Nations, The Sustainable Development Goals Report 2019
Photo: Josiah Brown, SIM USA

32 million girls of primary school age
are out of school
Source: United Nations,
Photo: Mike Knell

Young women are nearly 90% more likely
to be out of secondary school than their counterparts
Source: United Nations,
Photo: Binny V A

9 in 10 children in Africa are not learning
the most basic reading and maths
Source: United Nations
Photo: Feed My Starving Children

1 in 5 children, adolescents and youth
is out of school
Source: UNESCO
Photo: Marc Wathieu

53% of adolescents of upper secondary school age,
from 15-17 years, are out of school
Source: UNICEF
Photo: Thomas Galvez

The global number of students at the tertiary education level
rose from about 160 million in 2008
to about 200 million in 2015
Source: Yale University
Photo: John Walker

617 million youth worldwide
lack basic mathematics and literacy skills
Source: United Nations
Photo: Keith Ellwood

In 2018, one fifth of the world's youth were not engaged
in either education, employment or training
Source: United Nations Statistics Division
Photo: Martin Mutch

24.9 million people work under modern slavery conditions
Source: Global Slavery Index
Photo: Ty Chan, USAID

Labor market insecurity in developed countries is around 33% higher than when first measured, in 2007

Source: Organization for Economic Cooperation and Development

Photo: David Reece

Only 35% of children worldwide
receive social protection benefits
Source: United Nations, The Sustainable Development Goals Report 2019
Photo: Al Jazeera

152 million children aged 5-17 were in child labor in 2016,
of which, 73 million were in hazardous work
Source: International Labour Organization
Photo: Rod Waddington

Almost half of all 152 million children
victims of child labour are aged 5-11 years
Source: International Labour Organization
Photo: Gideon

Since 2004, the number of trade union members
has decreased in more than 30 countries
Source: International Labour Organization
Photo: Dun.can

Nonviolent campaigns are twice as likely to achieve their goals
as violent campaigns, and it takes around 3.5% of the population
actively participating in the protests to ensure serious political change
Source: Erica Chenoweth, Harvard University
Photo: Patrice Calatayu

Across most of the world, the percentage of adults
that consider they have a great job rarely tops 10%
Source: Gallup
Photo: barockschloss

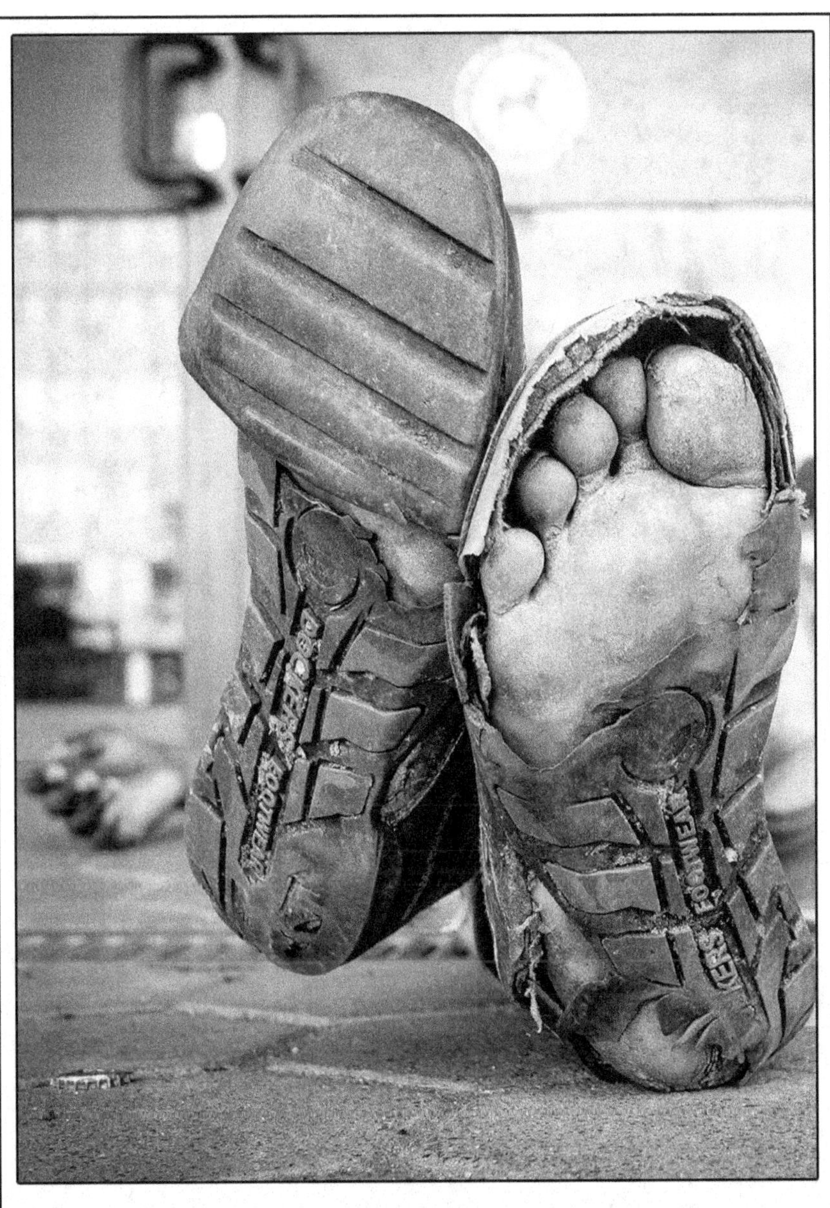

150 million people, or about 2% of the world's population,
are homeless
Source: United Nations
Photo: Karl-Heinz Kasper

Today, more people than ever before live in a country
other than the one in which they were born
Source: United Nations
Photo: TeaMeister

There are an estimated 244 million international migrants
and over 750 million internal migrants worldwide
Source: International Organization for Migration
Photo: Jonathan McIntosh

Today, there are more than 68.5 million
forcibly displaced people
Source: United Nations
Photo: Jonathan McIntosh

There are an estimated 1 billion internal migrants
in developing countries
Source: FAO
Photo: Michael Davis-Burchat

1/3 of all international migrants
are between the ages of 15 and 34
Source: FAO
Photo: George Martell

Women account for almost half of all
international migrants
Source: FAO
Photo: Mario Fornasari

About 70.8 million – one in every 108 people worldwide –
were displaced by conflict or persecution in 2018
Source: United Nations
Photo: EU Civil Protection and Humanitarian Aid

9 out of 10 refugees
are hosted by developing countries
Source: United Nations
Photo: Foreign and Commonwealth Office

Nearly one billion people around the world
have no form of legal identification
Source: World Bank
Photo: Denkrahm

More than 2/3 of countries score less than half
of the achievable score on the Corruption Perception Index
Source: Transparency International
Photo: Naberacka

Worldwide, nearly 6 in 10 people think that their government
is doing poorly fighting corruption in their country
Source: Transparency International
Photo: Master Steve Rapport

Only 1 in 3 people in developed countries feel they have
an influence over what their government does
Source: OECD
Photo: Bread for the World

Around 80% of subjects worldwide watch news on television
and 40% read newspapers
Source: Patrick Kennedy and Andrea Prat (Columbia University)
Photo: K. Kendall

The average level of trust in the news
fell to 42% in 2018
Source: Digital News Report 2019
Photo: Eric Bridiers, U.S. Mission Geneva

32% of people actively avoid watching the news
Source: Digital News Report 2019
Photo: Robert Anders

Plastic and cosmetic surgery procedures increased
from 14 million to over 23 million globally since 2010
Source: Insider
Photo: Paulina Jowita Koltun PJK

Individualism has increased by about
12% worldwide since 1960
Source: Association for Psychological Science
Photo: Dominic

In the last 4 decades, divorce rates
have more than doubled worldwide
Source: Social Forces
Photo: Ewan Munro

About 50 million induced abortions occurr worldwide each year
Source: World Health Organization
Photo: katieg93

There are 3.2 billion daily active
social media users worldwide
Source: Emarsys
Photo: Joey Zanotti

More than 1.5 billion people use Facebook every day
Source: Social Media Today
Photo: aisletwentytwo

60% of links are shared without ever being clicked
Source: Columbia University and French National Institute
Photo: Fouquier

2.7 times higher rates of depression were found
in frequent social media users over less frequent users
Source: University of Pittsburgh School of Medicine
Photo: Tomas Forgac

49% of people rely on influencer recommendations
to make a purchase
Source: Annalect and Twitter
Photo: Beckie

The daily estimated brand exposure of a person living in a city
has risen from 2,000 thirty years ago to up to 5,000 today
Source: Yankelovich, Inc.
Photo: José Elias

62% of shoppers make a purchase
to achieve a psychological reward
Source: TNS Global
Photo: Sigfrid Lundberg

Women account for 85% of all consumer purchases
Source: Yankelovich, Inc.
Photo: Marco Monetti

Almost 40% of millennials went into debt
in order to keep up with friends
Source: Credit Karma and Qualtrics
Photo: Ralf Scherer

Government restrictions on religion and social hostilities
involving religion have increased more than 20% since 2007
Source: Pew Research Center
Photo: Coastal Elite

1.2 billion people in the world, or 16%, don't identify with
or practise an organised religion
Source: Pew Research Center
Photo: Bradley Weber

Close to 800,000 people die due to suicide every year
Source: World Health Organization
Photo: Petras Gagilas

Suicide is the second leading cause of death
among 15–29-year-olds
Source: World Health Organization
Photo: Kelsey Graeter

NATURAL & UNNATURAL ENVIRONMENT

The age of the Earth
is estimated to be 4.54 billion years
Source: Scientific American
Photo: NASA

The ocean covers some 72% of the Earth's surface
Source: United Nations
Photo: Nick Harris

The ocean absorbs about 30% of human emissions
of carbon dioxide from fossil fuel burning
cement production, deforestation and other land use change
Source: United Nations
Photo: Andrew

Ocean acidity has increased by 26%
since pre-industrial times
Source: United Nations, The Sustainable Development Goals Report 2019
Photo: Neil Williamson

Today, sea level is 5 to 8 inches (13-20 centimeters)
higher on average than it was in 1900
Source: Smithsonian Institution
Photo: Guillaume Baviere

During the last 4 decades, 75% of the sea level rise can be
attributed to glacier mass loss and ocean thermal expansion
Source: United Nations
Photo: Michael Gwyther-Jones

Only 2.5% of all the water on Earth is freshwater
Source: IAEA
Photo: ufoncz

Less than 1% of the Earth's freshwater
is usable and available for ecosystems and humans
Source: IAEA
Photo: Kandukuru Nagarjun

68.6% of the world's freshwater
is in the form of ice and permanent snow in mountains
Source: IAEA
Photo: Liam Quinn

The Arctic's sea ice extent has shrunk in every successive
decade since 1979, with 1.07 million km² of ice loss every decade
Source: United Nations
Photo: Smudge 9000

Antarctica lost as much sea ice between 2014 and 2018
as the Arctic lost in 34 years
Source: NASA
Photo: Jasmine Nears

Global consumption of water is doubling every 20 years,
more than twice the rate of human population growth
Source: FAO
Photo: Steffen Zahn

Only about 15% of the world's population
enjoys relative abundance of water
Source: IAEA
Photo: Evan Blaser

Only 8% of freshwater withdrawals is for domestic use
Source: IAEA
Photo: Thierry Leclerc

Over 2 billion people live in countries
experiencing high water stress
Source: United Nations, 2018
Photo: Tim J Keegan

About 4 billion people experience severe water scarcity
during at least one month of the year
Source: United Nations, The Sustainable Development Goals Report 2019
Photo: Julien Harneis

By 2025, half of the world's population
will be living in water-stressed areas
Source: World Health Organization
Photo: Patrick Emerson

1/3 of the world's biggest groundwater systems
are already in distress
Source: United Nations, The Sustainable Development Goals Report 2019
Photo: James St. John

The agriculture sector accounts for nearly
70% of global freshwater withdrawals
Source: United Nations, The Sustainable Development Goals Report 2019
Photo: Lance Cheung, USDA

Freshwater species numbers
show an 83% decline since 1970
Source: World Wide Fund For Nature, Living Planet Report 2018
Photo: Julia Maudlin

Humankind has permanently altered the flow
of more than 93% of the world's rivers
Source: UN Environment
Photo: Gordon Wrigley

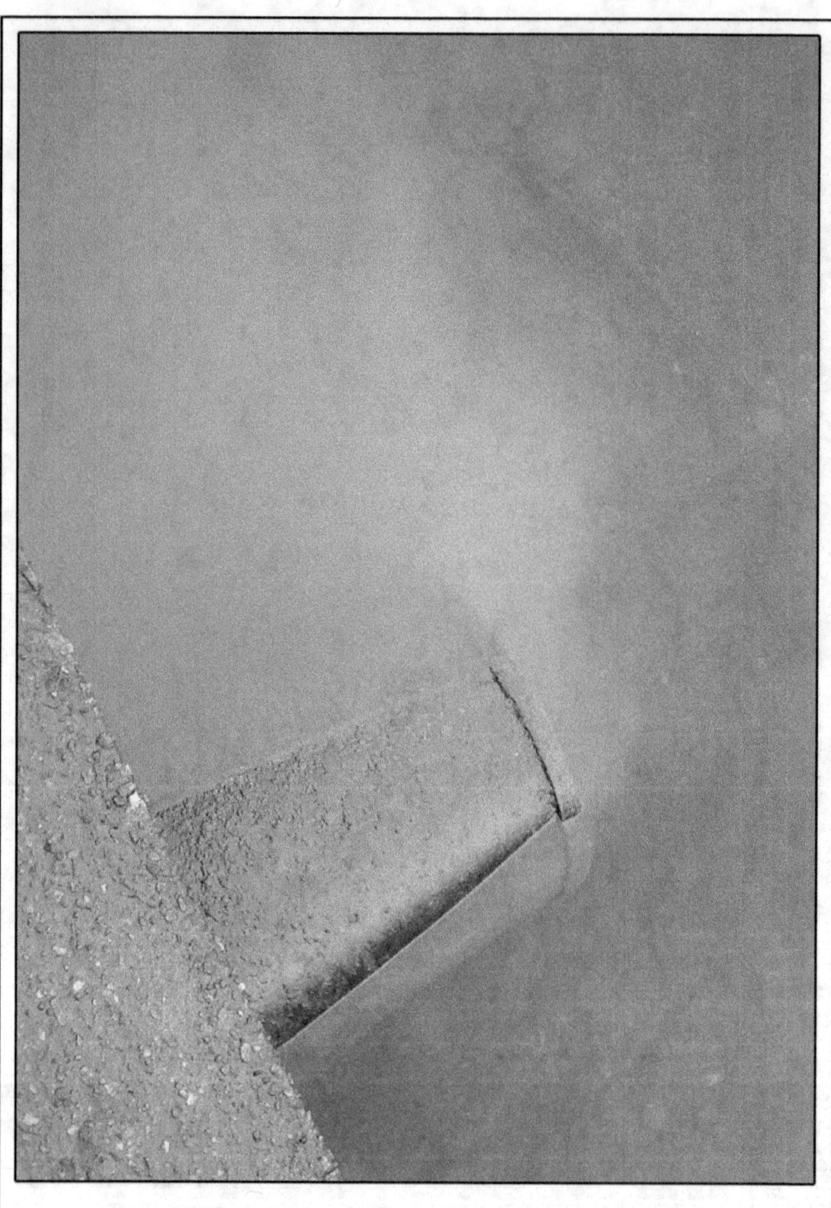

About 90% of wastewater in cities in developing countries
is discharged untreated directly into rivers, lakes or the ocean
Source: UNEP
Photo: Murray Barnes

Almost 6 billion tonnes of fish and invertebrates
have been taken from the world's oceans since 1950
Source: World Wide Fund For Nature, Living Planet Report 2018
Photo: Hernán Piñera

Overfishing has reduced some commercial fish stocks
by more than 90%
Source: International Union for Conservation of Nature
Photo: Garry Knight

An estimated 27% of landed fish is lost or wasted between
landing and consumption
Source: United Nations
Photo: Paulo Valdivieso

There are about 2.8 million
motorized fishing vessels in the world
Source: WWF, Living Planet Report
Photo: Andrew

Coral reefs support more than a quarter of marine life
but the world has already lost about half
of its shallow water corals in only 30 years
Source: World Wide Fund For Nature, Living Planet Report 2018
Photo: Julie Bedford, NOAA

Nearly 200 million people depend on coral reefs
to protect them from storm surges and waves
Source: World Wide Fund For Nature, Living Planet Report 2018
Photo: Laika ac

Clearing for development as well as over-exploitation and aquaculture
have contributed to a decline in the extent of mangroves
by 30% to 50% over the past 50 years
Source: World Wide Fund For Nature, Living Planet Report 2018
Photo: hds

The world has lost 70% of its natural wetlands
over the last century
Source: United Nations, The Sustainable Development Goals Report 2019
Photo: USFWS Mountain-Prairie

40% of the world's oxygen
is produced by rainforests
Source: International Union for Conservation of Nature (IUCN)
Photo: Mike Goren

1.6 billion people depend on forests
Source: International Union for Conservation of Nature (IUCN)
Photo: Stonestreet's Coaches

Tropical, temperate and boreal forests cover only 30% of the Earth's land area, and yet they are home to more than 80% of all terrestrial species of animals, plants and insects
Source: International Union for Conservation of Nature (IUCN)
Photo: Andy Hay

Almost 20% of the Amazon rainforest
has disappeared in just 50 years
Source: World Wide Fund For Nature, Living Planet Report 2018
Photo: Neil Palmer, CIAT

There are about 3 trillion trees in the world
Source: Nature
Photo: Dominic

Over 15 billlion trees are cut down each year
Source: Nature
Photo: Counselman Collection

The global number of trees has fallen by approximately
46% since the start of human civilization
Source: Nature
Photo: Tony Hisgett

Over half the trees cut down worldwide
are burnt to produce charcoal
Source: United Nations
Photo: TREEAID

Land degradation seriously impacts 75% of terrestrial
ecosystems, reducing the welfare of more than 3 billion people
Source:: WWF, Living Planet Report 2018
Photo: LiveWildPhotos

Nearly 1/3 of the world's cropland has been abandoned
in the past 40 years because of erosion
Source:: ,United Nations Development Programme
Photo: Hernán Piñera

Humankind has deliberately modified
more than 75% of the planet's land surface
Source: UN Environment
Photo: Geoff Parsons

There has been a 30% decline in biodiversity health since 1970
Source: World Wildlife Fund
Photo: Theo Crazzolara

There has been a 60% drop in populations of mammals,
birds, fish, reptiles and amphibians over the past 40 years
Source:: WWF, Living Planet Report 2018
Photo: Bob Dass

Current rates of species extinctions
are 100 to 1,000 times higher
than before human pressure became a prominent factor
Source: WWF, Living Planet Index 2018
Photo: Neil McIntosh

Of all the plant, amphibian, reptile, bird and mammal species
that have gone extinct since AD 1500, 75% were harmed
by overexploitation or agricultural activity or both
Source: World Wide Fund For Nature, Living Planet Report 2018
Photo: Christopher Griner

Since agriculture began about 12,000 years ago,
roughly 7,000 plant species have been used
for human consumption
Source: International Union for Conservation of Nature
Photo: USDA NRCS Montana

There are between 50,000 and 75,000 known
medicinal and aromatic plants used industrially
Source: IUCN Medicinal Plants Specialist Group
Photo: Marco Verch

Palm oil is now the world's most produced,
consumed and traded vegetable oil
Source: World Wide Fund For Nature, Living Planet Report 2018
Photo: Tatters

Wheat is the most widely grown crop in the world
and provides 20% of the daily protein and of the
food calories for 4.5 billion people
Source: FAO
Photo: Stanze

80% of agricultural land is used for livestock feed
Source: UN Environment
Photo: Stuart Richards

About 1/3 of the crops produced globally
are used to feed livestock
Source: FAO
Photo: Dave

The combined total of chickens, cows, sheep and pigs living
at any one time is 3 times higher than the number of people
Source: World Economic Forum
Photo: Mario Fornasari

An estimated 50 billion chickens
are slaughtered for food every year
Source: World Economic Forum
Photo: Lance Cheung, USDA

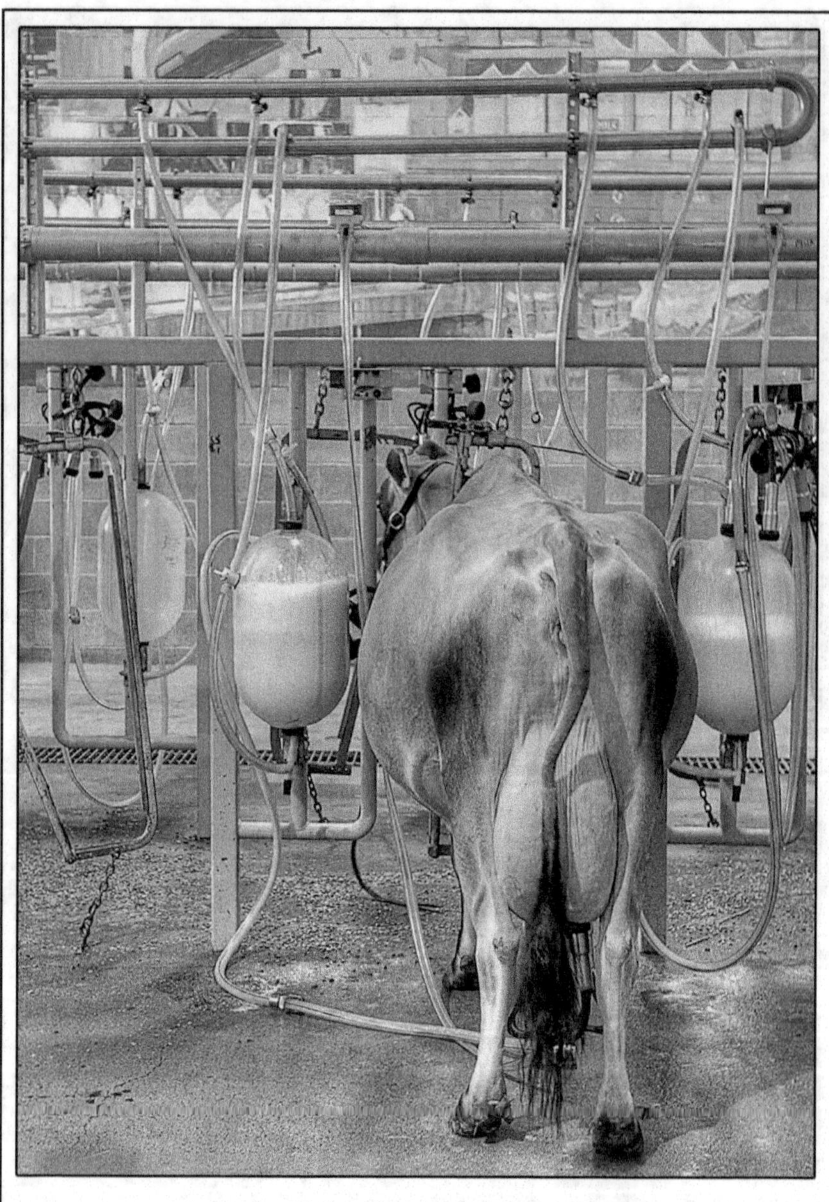

In the last 3 decades, world milk production
has increased by more than 58%
Source: FAO
Photo: Glen Bledsoe

There are more than 1000 pesticides used around the world
Source: World Health Organization
Photo: CIAT

About 87% of all flowering plant species are pollinated
by animals, and crops that are partially pollinated by animals
account for 35% of global food production
Source: Wide Fund For Nature, Living Planet Report 2018
Photo: Tom Shockey

Over the past 50 years, our consumption of natural resources
has increased by about 190%
Source: Global Footprint Network. National Footprint Accounts 2018 edition
Photo: Bureau of Land Management California

Less than 10% of the resources used by humanity
is put back into the economy
Source: UN Environment
Photo: Alan Levine

Roughly 1/3 of the food produced in the world
for human consumption every year gets lost or wasted
Source: Food and Agriculture Organization (FAO)
Photo: U.S. Department of Agriculture

56% of all food waste is generated in high-income countries
Source: UN Environment
Photo: Taz

Although they only account for 16% of the world's population,
high-income countries combined are generating
more than 1/3 of the world's waste
Source: World Bank
Photo: Tiomax80

The world generates at least 3.5 million tons of plastic
and other solid waste a day,
10 times the amount a century ago
Source: World Bank
Photo: ACE Solid Waste

Electronic waste amounted to about 50 million tons in 2018,
nearly a 50% increase in under a decade
Source: UN Environment
Photo: Stuart Richards

Up to 90% of electronic waste is illegally traded
or dumped each year
Source: UN Environment
Photo: Rwanda Green Fund

The treatment and disposal of waste generates
about 5% of global carbon dioxide emissions
Source: WARC
Photo: Kema Keur

The livestock sector contributes
14.5% of global greenhouse gas emissions
Source: FAO
Photo: elzoh

Around 60 million barrels of petroleum product
move each day on the seas globally
Source: U.S. Energy Information Administration
Photo: Padraic

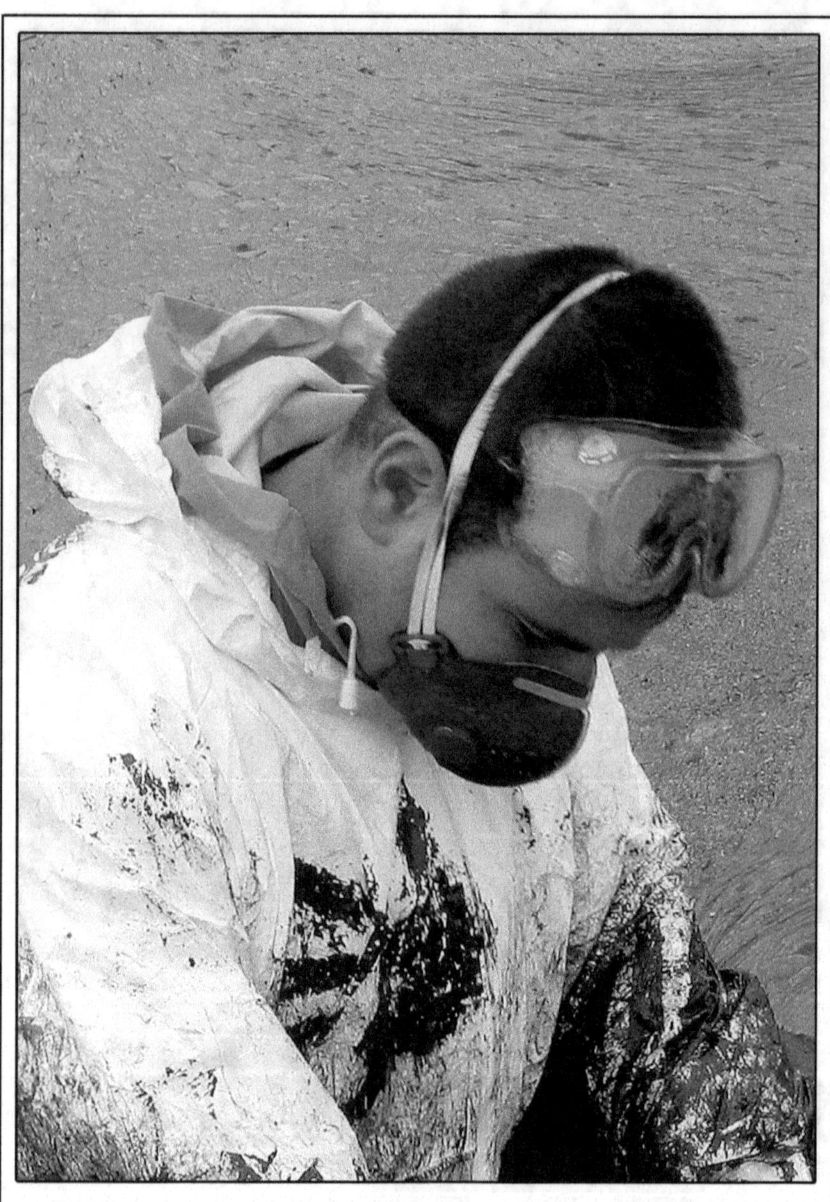

From 1970 to 2018, approximately 5.86 million tons of oil
have been lost as a result of tanker accidents
Source: International Tanker Owners Pollution Federation Limited
Photo: Stéphane M. Grueso

Nearly half of all plastic ever manufactured
has been made since 2000
Source: Roland Geyer, University of California, Santa Barbara
Photo: ikeofspain

40% of plastic produced is packaging,
used just once and then discarded
Source: Roland Geyer, University of California, Santa Barbara
Photo: Bo Eide

Since the 1960s, global demand for single-use plastic
has increased twenty-fold
Source: Morgan Stanley
Photo: Mike

Nearly a million plastic beverage bottles
are sold every minute around the world
Source: Euromonitor International
Photo: Shafiu Hussain

Every year, an estimated 8 million tons of plastic waste
end up in the world's oceans
Source: UN Environment
Photo: Peretz Partensky

Less than 1/5
of all plastic is recycled globally
Source: Roland Geyer, University of California, Santa Barbara
Photo: Andrew Bowden

Energy is the dominant contributor to climate change, accounting
for around 60% of total global greenhouse gas emissions
Source: United Nations, The Sustainable Development Goals Report 2019
Photo: glasseyes view

Nuclear energy provides about 11% of the world's electricity
from about 450 power reactors
Source: World Nuclear Association
Photo: Bjoern Schwarz

Global nuclear power generation increased in 2018
for the sixth straight year
Source: World Nuclear Association
Photo: Greg Dunlap

Coal-based power generation remains the largest source
of electricity generation worldwide, with a share of 38%
Source: International Energy Agency
Photo: Arnold Paul

Atmospheric carbon dioxide concentration is 146%
of pre-industrial levels
Source: United Nations, The Sustainable Development Goals Report 2019
Photo: Kim Hansen

In April 2018, levels of carbon dioxide in the atmosphere
reached the highest level in at least 800,000 years
Soure: Scripps Institute of Oceanography
Photo: Nevalenx

Global CO2 emissions from fuel combustion
increased by around 40% since 2000
Source: International Energy Agency (IEA)
Photo: Jules & Jenny

17.5% of total final energy consumption
came from renewable energy in 2015
Source: United Nations, The Sustainable Development Goals Report 2019
Photo: Baker County Tourism

Nearly 2/3 of all new power generation capacity
added in 2018 was from renewables
Source: International Renewable Energy Agency
Photo: Guilhem Vellut

Global investments in renewable energy
increased five-fold between 2004 and 2018
Source: International Institute for Sustainable Development (IISD)
Photo: Mark Floyd, Oregon State University

Electricity makes up only 20% of final energy use;
80% is concentrated in the heat and transport sectors
Source: United Nations Statistics Division
Photo: Christian

There are more than 1.4 billion vehicles in use worldwide
Source: International Organization of Motor Vehicle Manufacturers
Photo: joiseyshowaa

The global road network
covers over 30 million kilometers
Source: CIA, The World Factbook
Photo: Benedict Adam

The global rail network encompasses
over 1 million route kilometers
Source: International Union of Railways
Photo: Gary Bembridge

55% of the world's population
lives in urban areas
Source: United Nations Population Division
Photo: joiseyshowaa

Cities and metropolitan areas account for about 70% of global
carbon emissions and over 60% of resource use
Source: United Nations, The Sustainable Development Goals Report 2019
Photo: Janne Räkköläinen

Developing countries account for 93% of urbanization globally,
40% of which is the expansion of slums
Source: UN-Habitat
Photo: Aleksandr Zykov

China was home to 80% of urban growth in East Asia
from 2000-2010
Source: World Bank
Photo: Jakob Montrasio

The number of megacities (more than 10 million inhabitants)
has grown from 2 in 1950 to over 30 today
Source: United Nations
Photo: Dani

64% of the world's cities exceed
the World Health Organization's annual exposure guideline
for PM2.5 fine particulate matter
Source: Greenpeace and AirVisual
Photo: Eileen MacAvery

9 out of 10 urban residents
breathe polluted air
Source: United Nations, The Sustainable Development Goals Report 2019
Photo: Gauthier Delecroix

22 of the world's 30 most polluted cities
are in India
Source: Greenpeace and AirVisual
Photo: Bill Bourne

Since 1800, global population has grown sevenfold,
surpassing 7.6 billion,
whereas the global economy has grown 30-fold
Source:: WWF, Living Planet Report 2018
Photo: Janko Luin

Developing countries are home
to 83% of the global population
Source: International Telecommunication Union
Photo: Tony Tarry

Almost 2/3 of the world's cities with populations
of over 5 million are located in areas at risk of sea level rise
Source: United Nations
Photo: William Warby

More than 600 million people live in coastal areas
that are less than 10 meters above sea level
Source: United Nations
Photo: baldeaglebluff

About 50% of all international tourists travel to coastal areas
Source: United Nations
Photo: Ana Lauriano Lauriano

The global mean temperature in 2018 was approximately
1°C above the pre-industrial baseline
Source: United Nations
Photo: Mike McBey

In the last 50 years, global average temperature
has risen at 170 times the background rate
Source: World Wide Fund For Nature, Living Planet Report 2018
Photo: 16:9clue

Climate-related and geophisical disasters claimed
an estimated 1.3 million lives between 1998 and 2017
Source: United Nations
Photo: Hypnotica Studios Infinite

In the past 20 years, 90 % of major disasters were caused
by weather-related events
Source: International Union for Conservation of Nature (IUCN)
Photo: Nick Harris

Globally, the number of reported weather-related
natural disasters has more than tripled since the 1960s
Source: World Health Organization
Photo: TLV and more

On average, natural disasters cost 68,000 lives
and affect 218 million people every year
Source: EM-DAT
Photo: NASA

Since 1992, floods, droughts and storms
have affected over 4 billion people
Source: UNISDR
Photo: Alachua County

From 1998 to 2017, direct economic losses
from disasters were estimated at almost $3 trillion
Source: United Nations, The Sustainable Development Goals Report 2019
Photo: Wavian

Among the 10 worst disasters in terms of economic damage
(when expressed relative to GDP),
8 occurred in low- or middle-income countries
Source: United Nations, The Sustainable Development Goals Report 2019
Photo: Stephen Kennedy

An annual average of 21.5 million people
have been forcibly internally displaced
by sudden weather-related hazards since 2008
Source: United Nations
Photo: Jorge Intriago

Worldwide reported economic losses from earthquakes, volcanic
eruptions, floods, hurricanes and other climate-related disasters
surged to total nearly $2.9 trillion over the past 20 years
Source: United Nations
Photo: Patrick Emerson

On an average day in August, satellites typically detect
10,000 actively burning fires around the world
Source: NASA
Photo: Tim Vrieling

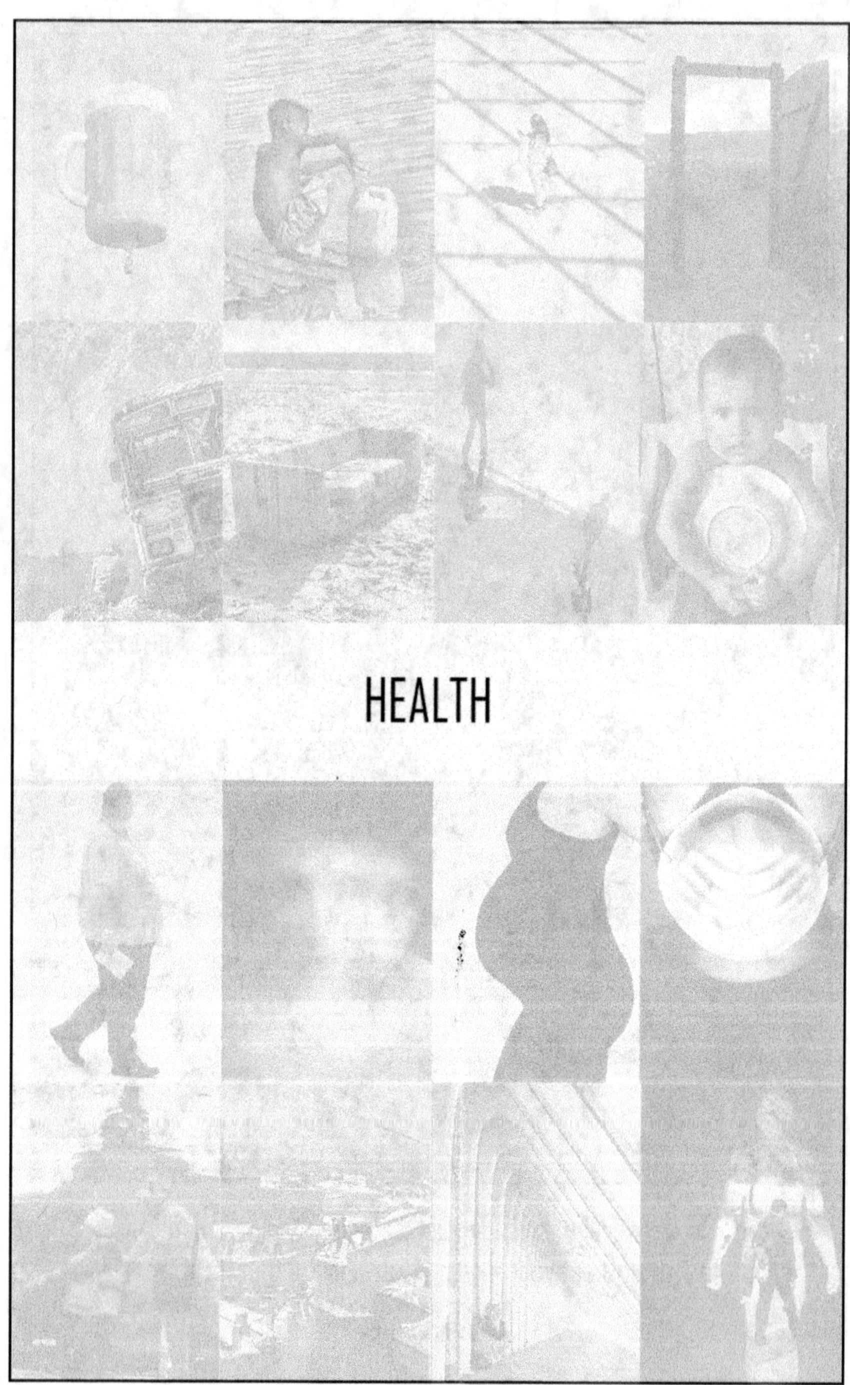

HEALTH

Global average life expectancy increased by 5.5 years
between 2000 and 2016, the fastest increase since the 1960s
Source: World Health Organization
Photo: Alexander Mueller

Global life expectancy at birth in 2016 was 72.0 years
(74.2 years for females and 69.8 years for males)
Source: World Health Organization
Photo: Timon Hast

Of the 40 leading causes of death, 33 causes contribute more
to reduced life expectancy in men than in women
Source: World Health Organization
Photo: Ramón Peco

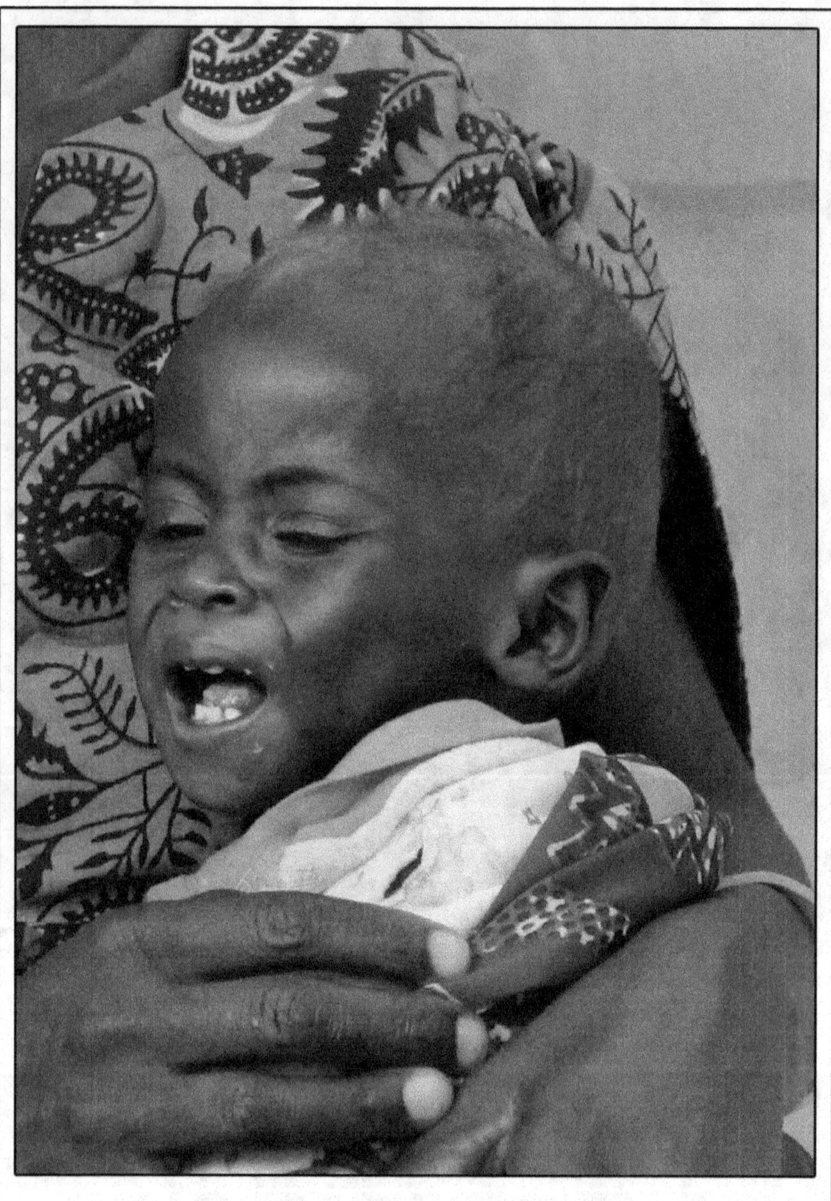

In low-income countries, almost 1 in 3 deaths
are in children aged under 5 years
Source: World Health Organization
Photo: Marisol Grandon, UK Department for International Development

More than 80% of the 2.5 million newborns
who die every year are of low birthweight
Source: World Health Organization
Photo: advencap

Maternal mortality is the second leading cause of death
for women of reproductive age worldwide
Source: World Health Organization
Photo: Emma Freeman

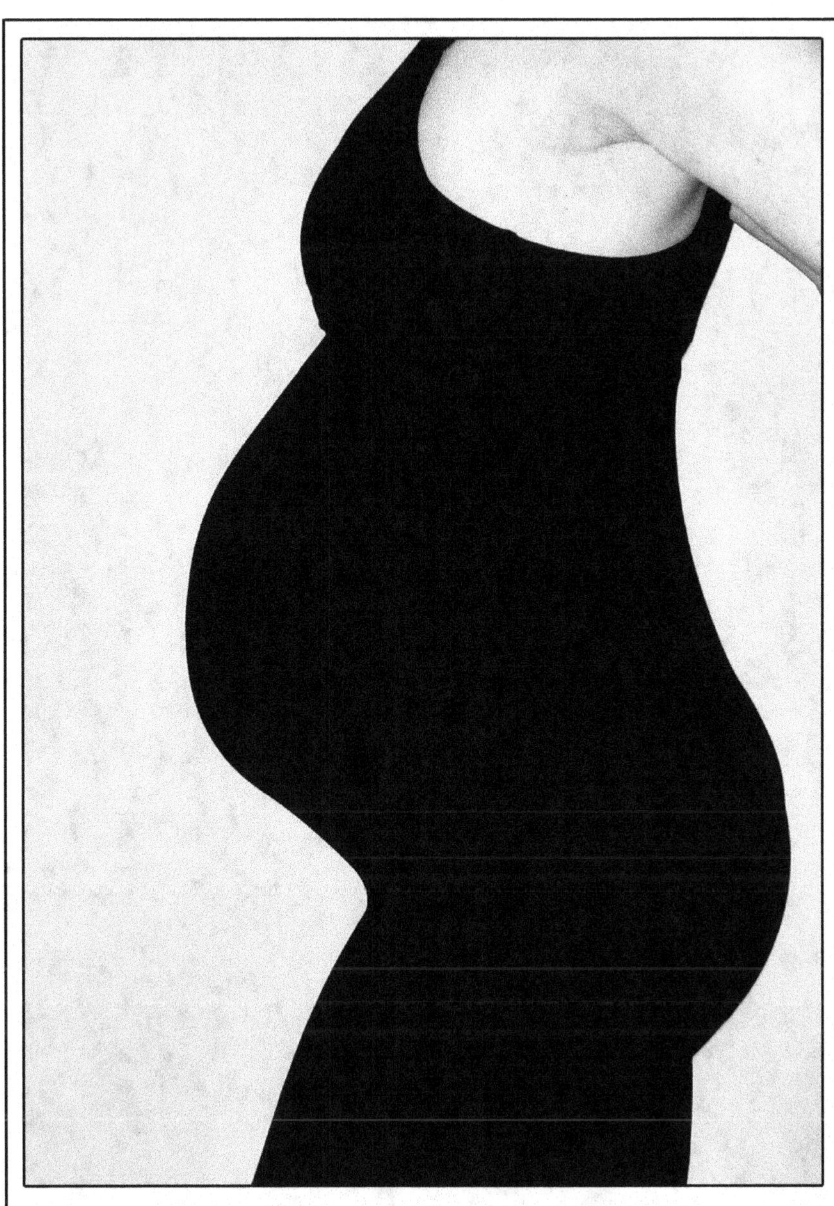

Since 2000, the number of babies born through
caesarean section almost doubled
Source: The Lancet
Photo: Jessica Ellis

Ischaemic heart disease and stroke have remained
the leading causes of death globally in the last 15 years
Source: World Health Organization
Photo: Funk Dooby

Cancer is the second leading cause of death worldwide
Source: World Health Organization
Photo: A Healthier Michigan

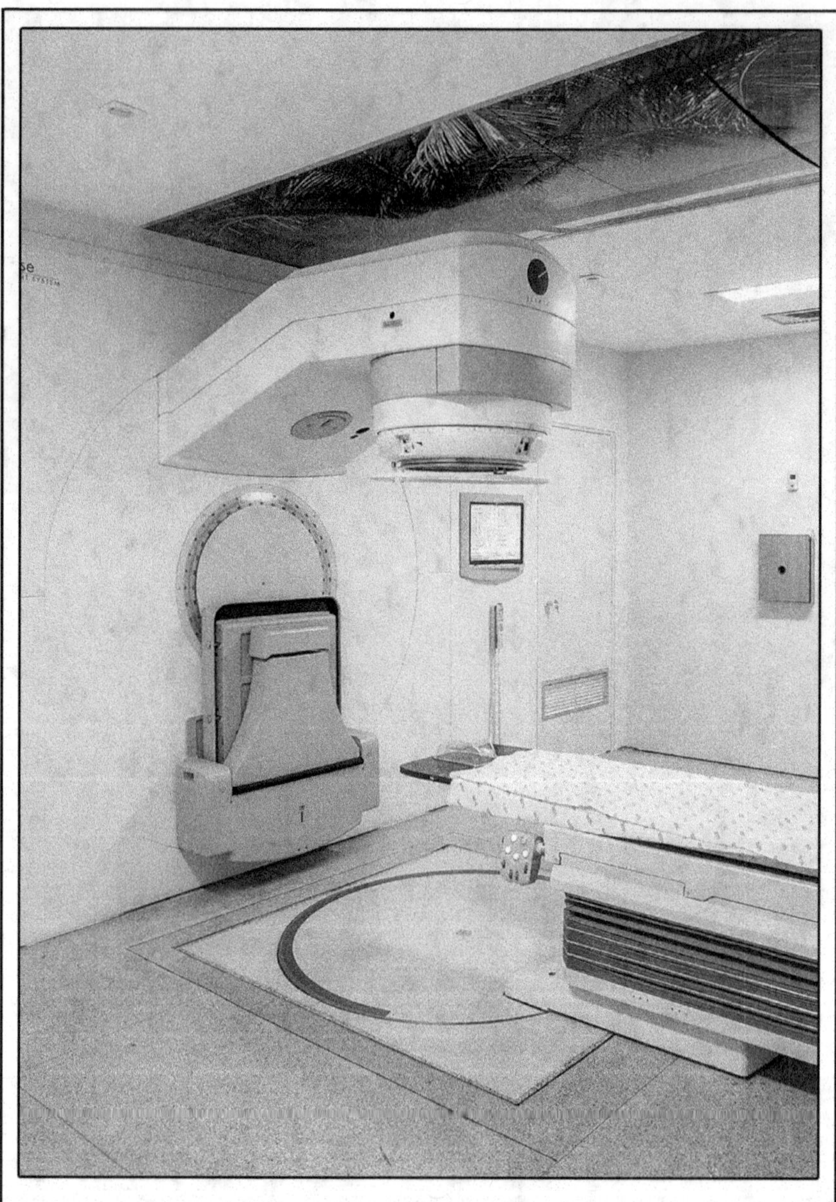

There were an estimated 18 million cancer cases
around the world in 2018
Source: World Cancer Research Fund International
Photo: Governo do Estado de São Paulo

The number of people suffering from hunger
has been on the rise since 2014
Source: United Nations, The Sustainable Development Goals Report 2019
Photo: Feed My Starving Children

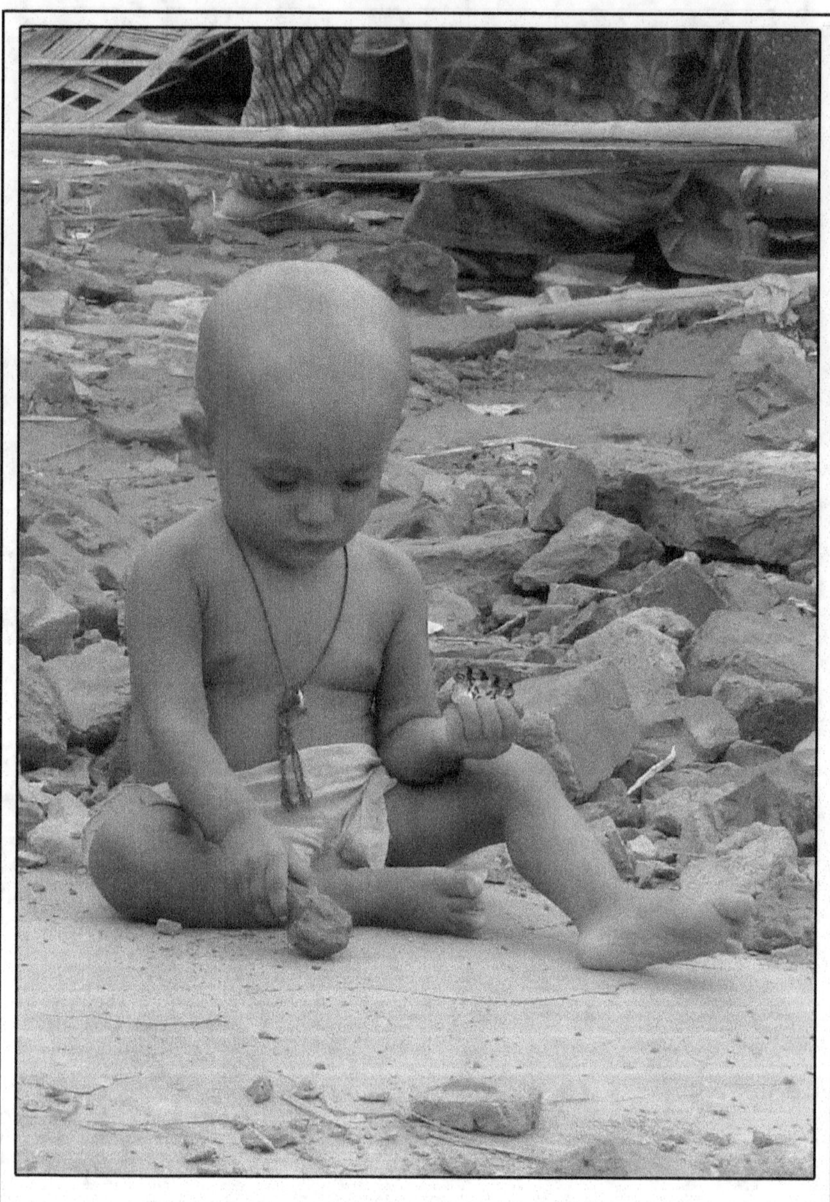

The Asia-Pacific region is home to more than 60%
of the world's undernourished
Source: FAO
Photo: Tareq Salahuddin

149 million children under 5 years of age
were chronically undernourished in 2018
Source: United Nations, The Sustainable Development Goals Report 2019
Photo: Paul Edgar Pastoral

Micronutrient deficiencies
affect some 2 billion people globally
Source: FAO
Photo: Rod Waddington

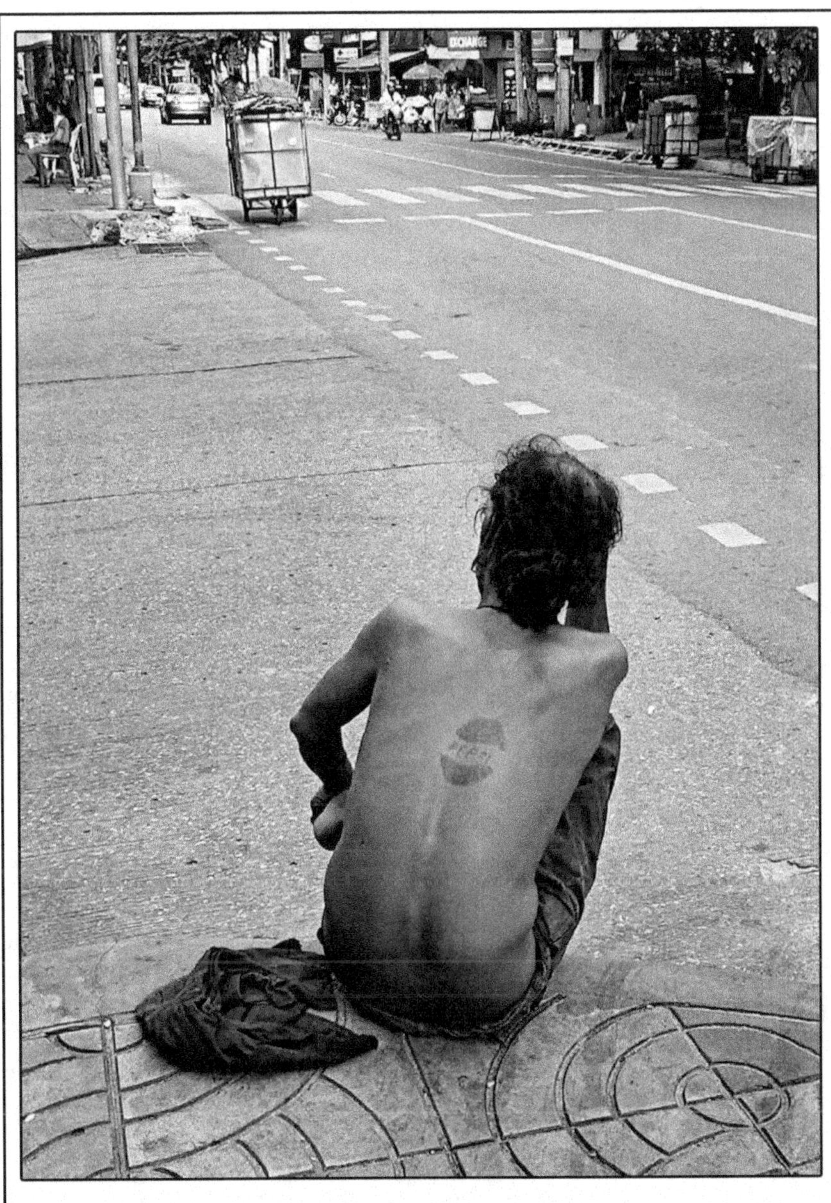

About 2 billion people do not have regular access
to nutritious and sufficient food
Source: Food and Agriculture Organization (FAO)
Photo: AK Rockefeller:

Animal-source foods currently comprise 39% of protein
and 18% of calorie intake worldwide
Source: FAO
Photo: Bob Nichols, USDA

3 billion people lack clean cooking fuels and technology
Source: United Nations, The Sustainable Development Goals Report 2019
Photo: Ben Grey

More than 600 million people fall ill and 420,000 die
every year as a result of eating food contaminated
with bacteria, viruses, parasites, toxins and chemicals
Source: FAO
Photo: Matthew Yglesias

Poor diets are linked to 20% of all deaths worldwide
Source: The Lancet
Photo: Hernán Piñera

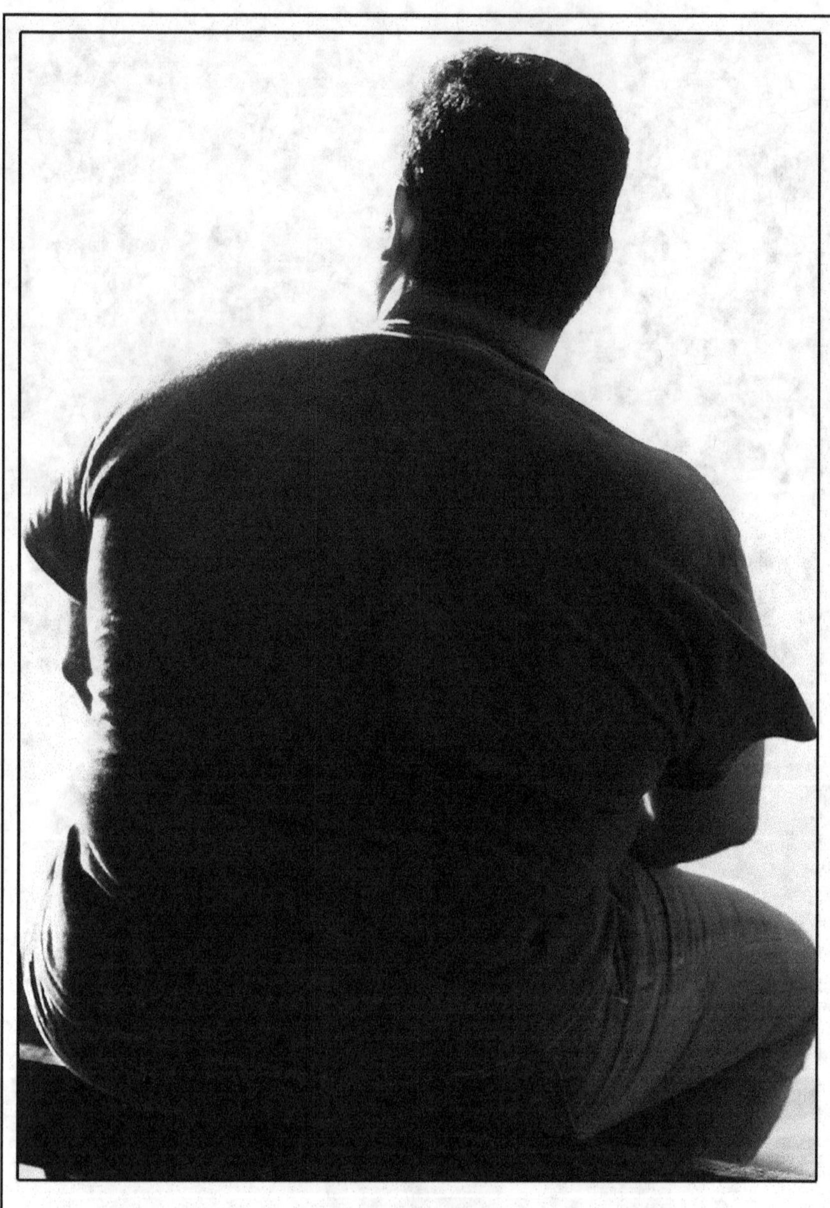

More than 1.9 billion adults, 18 years and older,
are overweight
Source: World Health Organization
Photo: GPS

40 million children under 5 are overweight
Source: United Nations, The Sustainable Development Goals Report 2019
Photo: Esin Üstün

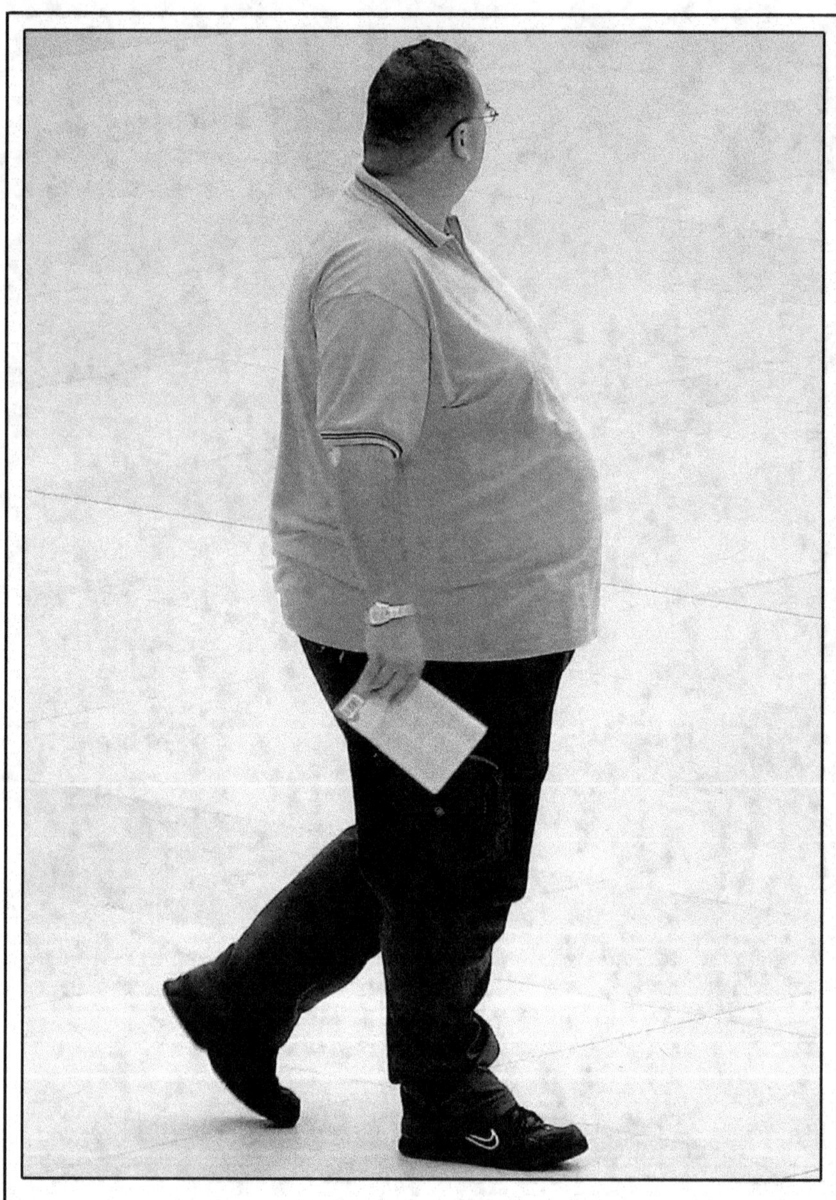

Worldwide obesity has nearly tripled since 1975
Source: World Health Organization
Photo: CGP Grey

The number of people with diabetes has increased
from 108 million in 1980 to more than 420 million today
Source: World Health Organization
Photo: Tebo Steele

60 to 85% of people in the world
lead sedentary lifestyles
Source: World Health Organization
Photo: Bob Dass

Approximately 2 million deaths per year
are attributed to physical inactivity
Source: World Health Organization
Photo: Dave Hosford

With no improvement in global levels since 2001,
1.4 billion adults do not meet recommended levels of activity
to stay healthy
Source: World Health Organization
Photo: Alexander Mueller

Globally, at least 2 billion people use a drinking water source
contaminated with faeces
Source: World Health Organization
Photo: Kandukuru Nagarjun

884 million people lack access to safe water supplies
Source: International Union for Conservation of Nature (IUCN)
Photo: Rod Waddington

2 out of 5 people worldwide do not have a
basic handwashing facility with soap and water at home
Source: United Nations, The Sustainable Development Goals Report 2019
Photo: Sonia Hoque (REACH)

4.5 billion people lack access
to safely managed sanitation
Source: United Nations, The Sustainable Development Goals Report 2019
Photo: Rahul Ingle

2 billion people do not have access
to waste collection services
Source: United Nations, The Sustainable Development Goals Report 2019
Photo: Gauthier Delecroix

3.8 million people die every year as a result of household
exposure to smoke from dirty cookstoves and fuels
Source: World Health Organization
Photo: Richard Evea

An estimated 12.6 million deaths each year are attributable
to unhealthy environments, nearly 1 in 4 of total global deaths
Source: World Health Organization
Photo: Duke Yeh

4.2 million people die every year as a result of exposure
to ambient (outdoor) air pollution
Source: World Health Organization
Photo: Gauthier Delecroix

There are around 1.1 billion smokers
in the world today
Source: World Health Organization
Photo: Georgie Pauwels

Tobacco kills more than 8 million people each year
Source: World Health Organization
Photo: Mathias

1 in 4 heavy smokers die
before their 65th birthday
Source: Statistics Netherlands & Netherlands Institute of Mental Health and Addiction
Photo: Michael

100 million people died from tobacco use
in the 20th century
Source: American Cancer Society
Photo: TMAB2003

38.3% of the world's population drinks alcohol
Source: World Health Organization
Photo: Karen Roe

The harmful use of alcohol is a causal factor
in more than 200 disease and injury conditions
Source: World Health Organization
Photo: Steve Banfield

The harmful use of alcohol
results in 3.3 million deaths each year
Source: World Health Organization
Photo: Barbara Eckstein

Alcohol is responsible for 5% of global deaths
Source: World Health Organization
Photo: Arty Guerillas

Some 31 million persons have drug use disorders
Source: World Health Organization
Photo: Hernán Piñera

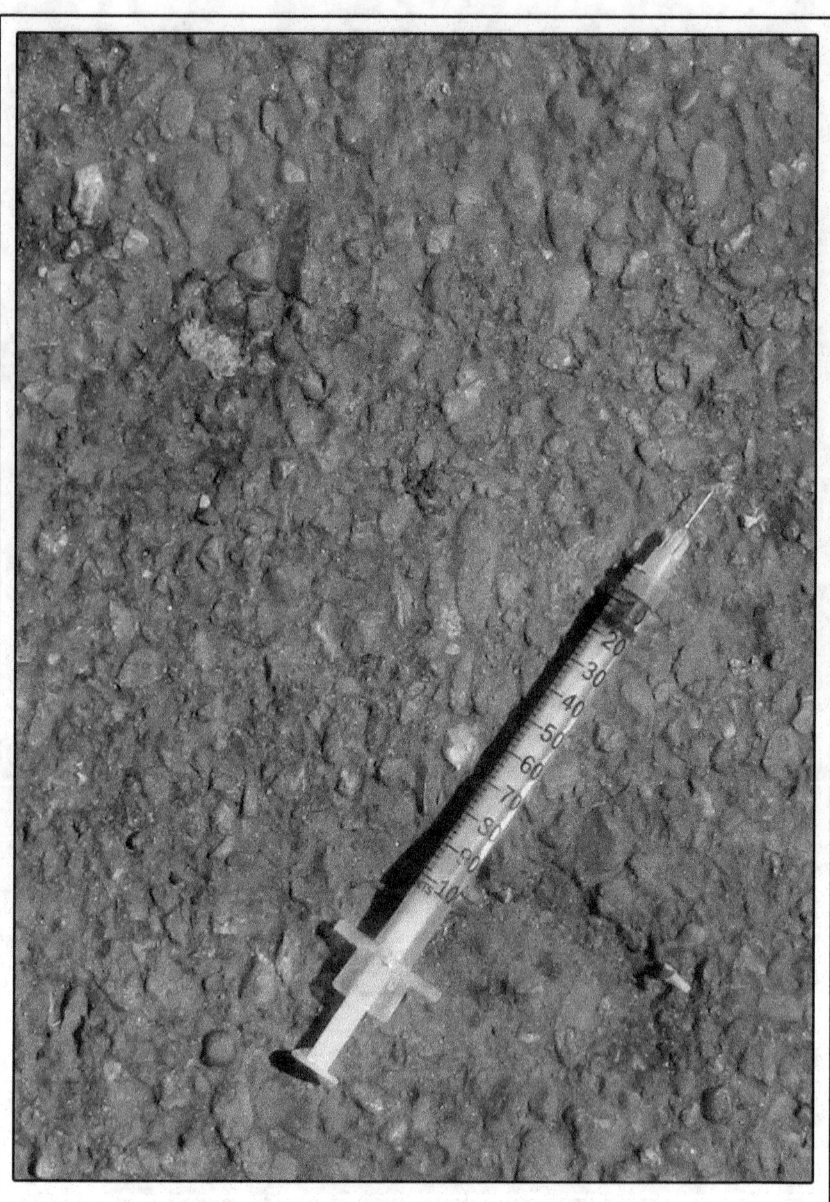

Since the year 2000, global deaths directly caused
by the use of drugs have increased more than 60%
Source: United Nations Office on Drugs and Crime
Photo: torbakhopper

Global opium and cocaine production
remain at a record high since 2017
Source: UNODC
Photo: Dr. Hans-Günter Wagner

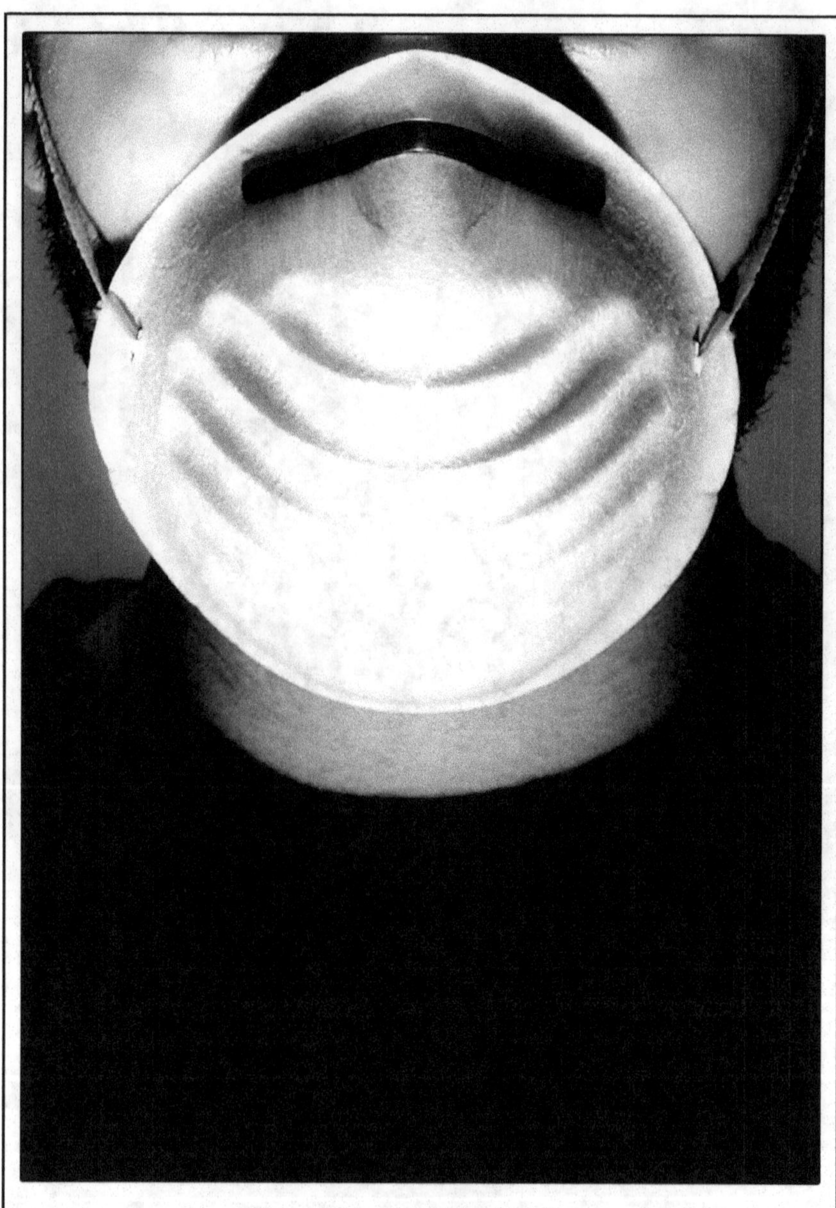

Allergic diseases affect the lives
of more than one billion people worldwide
Source: European Academy of Allergy and Clinical Immunology
Photo: B. Rosen

Asthma is the most common chronic illness
among children globally
Source: World Health Organization
Photo: Clint Budd

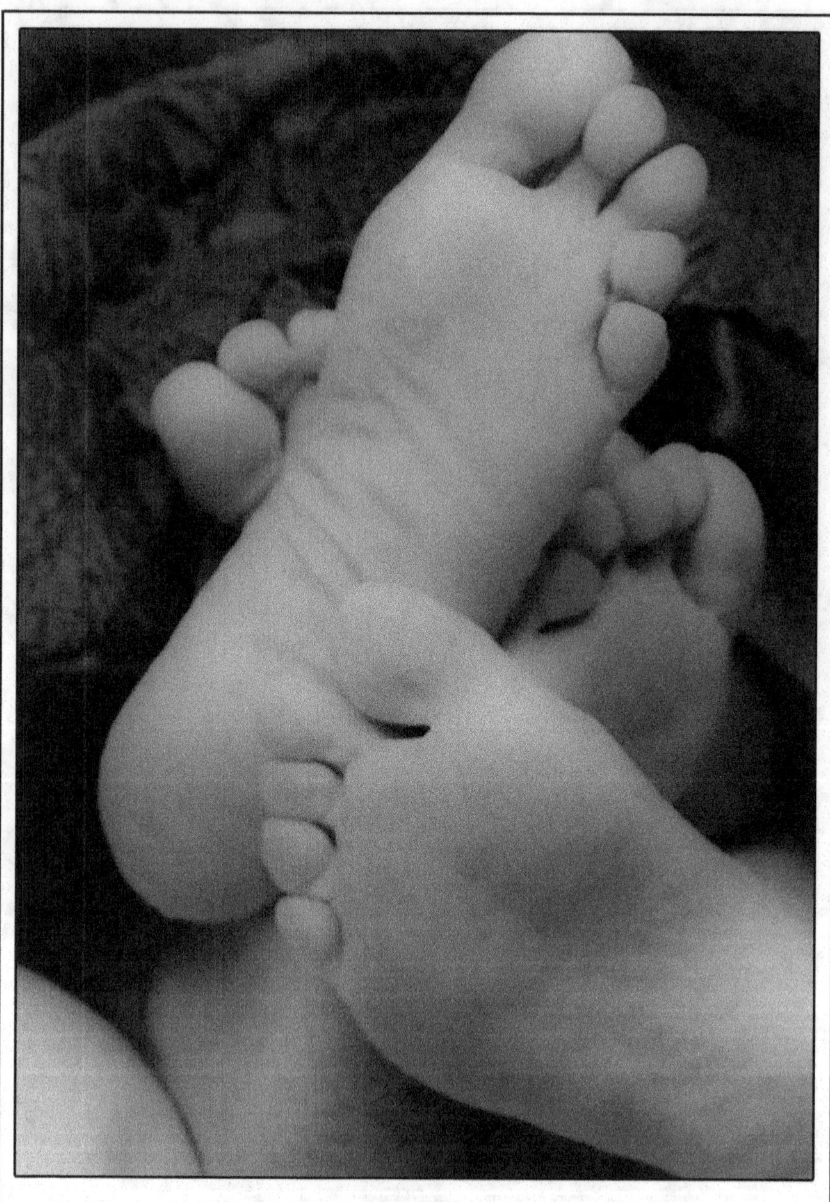

More than 1 million new sexually transmitted diseases occur
globally every day in people between the ages of 15 and 49
Source: World Health Organization
Photo: TR Haun

Since the early 1980s, HIV-related disease has claimed
35 million lives worldwide,
and today nearly 37 million people are living with HIV
Source: World Health Organization
Photo: Charlotte Nordahl

Nearly 1 billion people worldwide
have sleep apnea
Source: ResMed
Photo: Zach Dischner

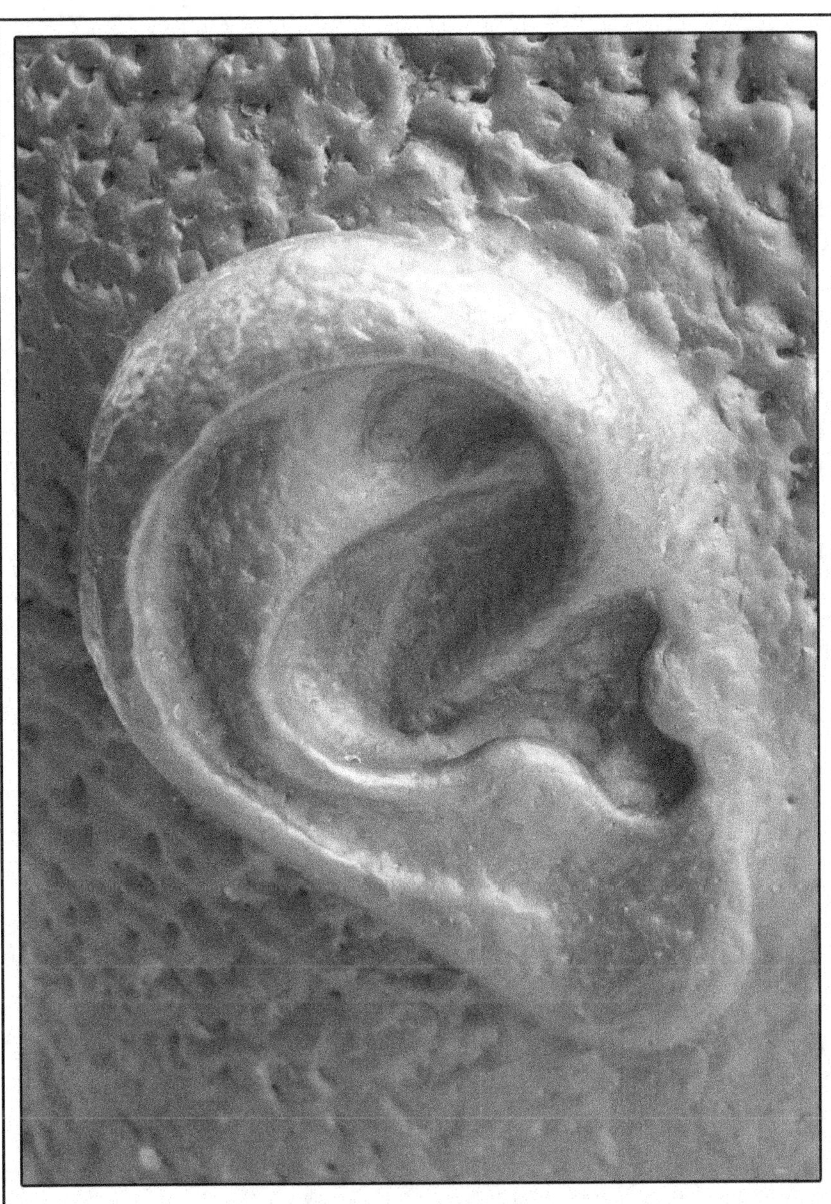

About 360 million people worldwide
suffer from hearing loss
Source: Hearing Health Foundation
Photo: Paul J Everett

Over 260 million people in the world are estimated
to be living with anxiety disorders
Source: World Health Organization
Photo: Jocelyn

Stress levels in the workplace are rising,
with 6 in 10 workers in major global economies
experiencing increased workplace stress
Source: The Regus Group
Photo: Seth Capitulo

More than 300 million people of all ages
suffer from depression
Source: World Health Organization
Photo: Matthew Miller

The bipolar affective disorder affects
about 60 million people worldwide
Source: World Health Organization
Photo: Maria Rantanen

58% of smartphone users don't go 1 hour
without checking their phones
Source: Mobile Mindset Study by Lookout
Photo: Ralf Steinberger

Young adults (age 15–24) check their smartphones
an average of 150 times per day
Source: New York Times
Photo: Edna Winti

374 million workers suffer non-fatal
occupational accidents every year
Source: International Labour Organization
Photo: Sergey Norin

2.78 million people die every year as the result of exposure
to safety and health hazards at work
Source: International Labour Organization
Photo: Regan Walsh

Road traffic accidents
constitute the 8th leading cause of death globally
Source: World Health Organization
Photo: Rajarshi Mitra

People with disabilities make up an estimated 1 billion,
or 15%, of the world's population
Source: International Labour Organization
Photo: Gauthier Delecroix

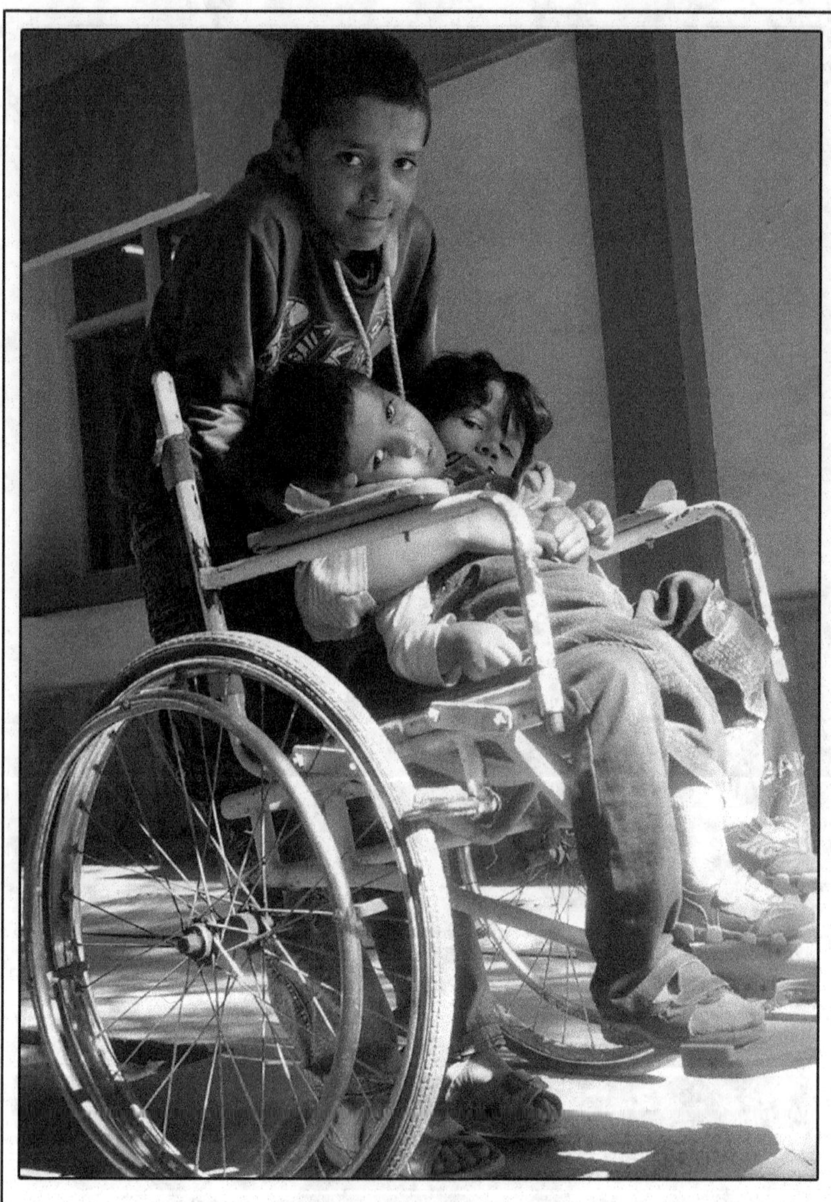

An estimated 93 million children around the world
live with disabilities
Source: UNICEF
Photo: Kanishka Afshari/FCO/DFID

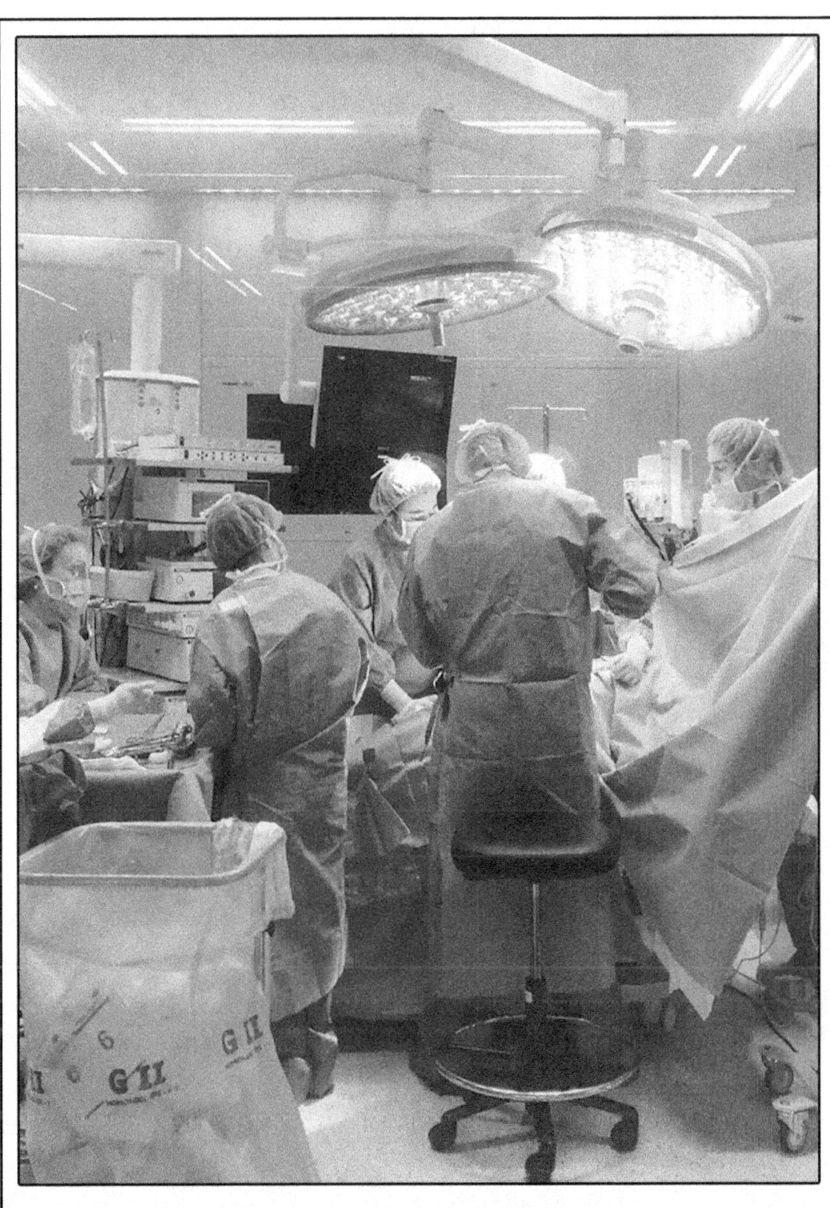

About 313 million surgical procedures
are performed worldwide every year
Source: The Lancet Commission on Global Surgery
Photo: Eduardo García Cruz

At least half of the world's population
lacks essential health services
Source: United Nations, The Sustainable Development Goals Report 2019
Photo: Sgt. James D. Sims, U.S. Army Africa

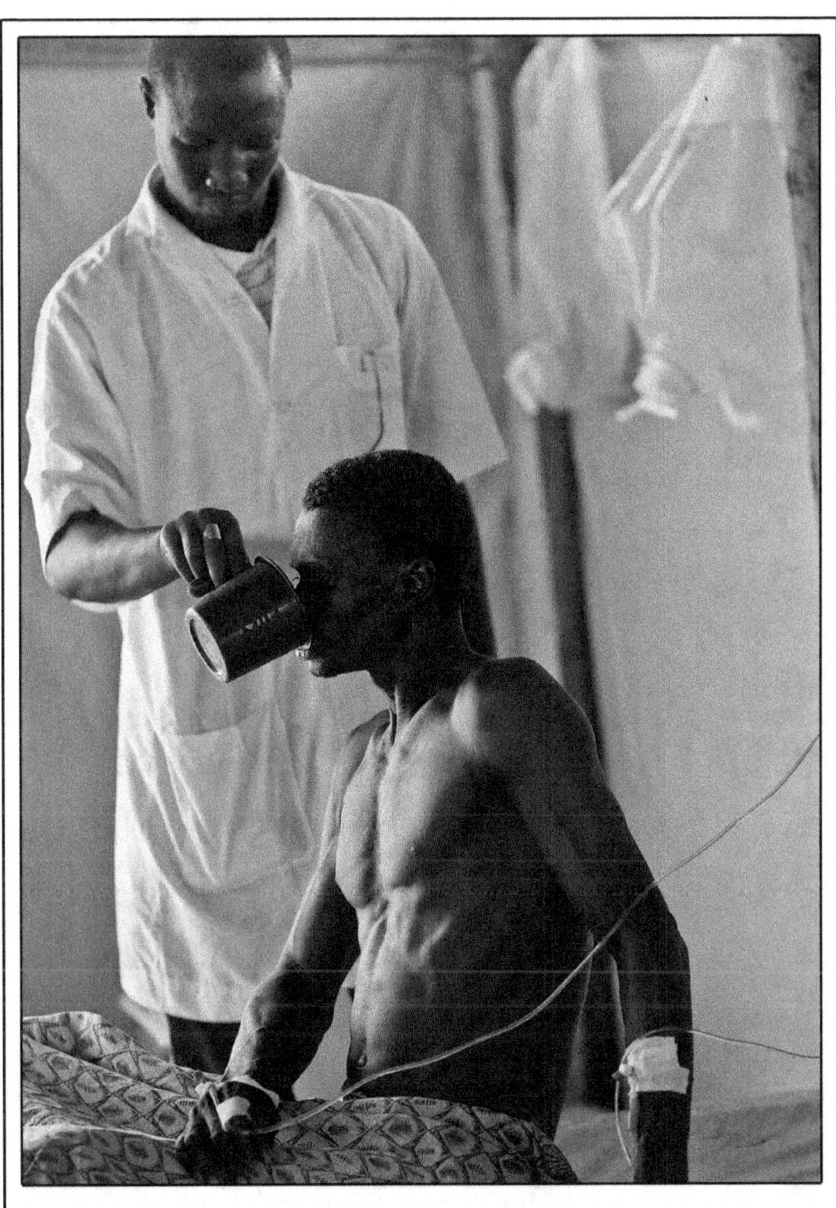

Close to 40% of all countries
have fewer than 10 medical doctors per 10,000 people
Source: United Nations, The Sustainable Development Goals Report 2019
Photo: Sean Smith, EU Civil Protection and Humanitarian Aid

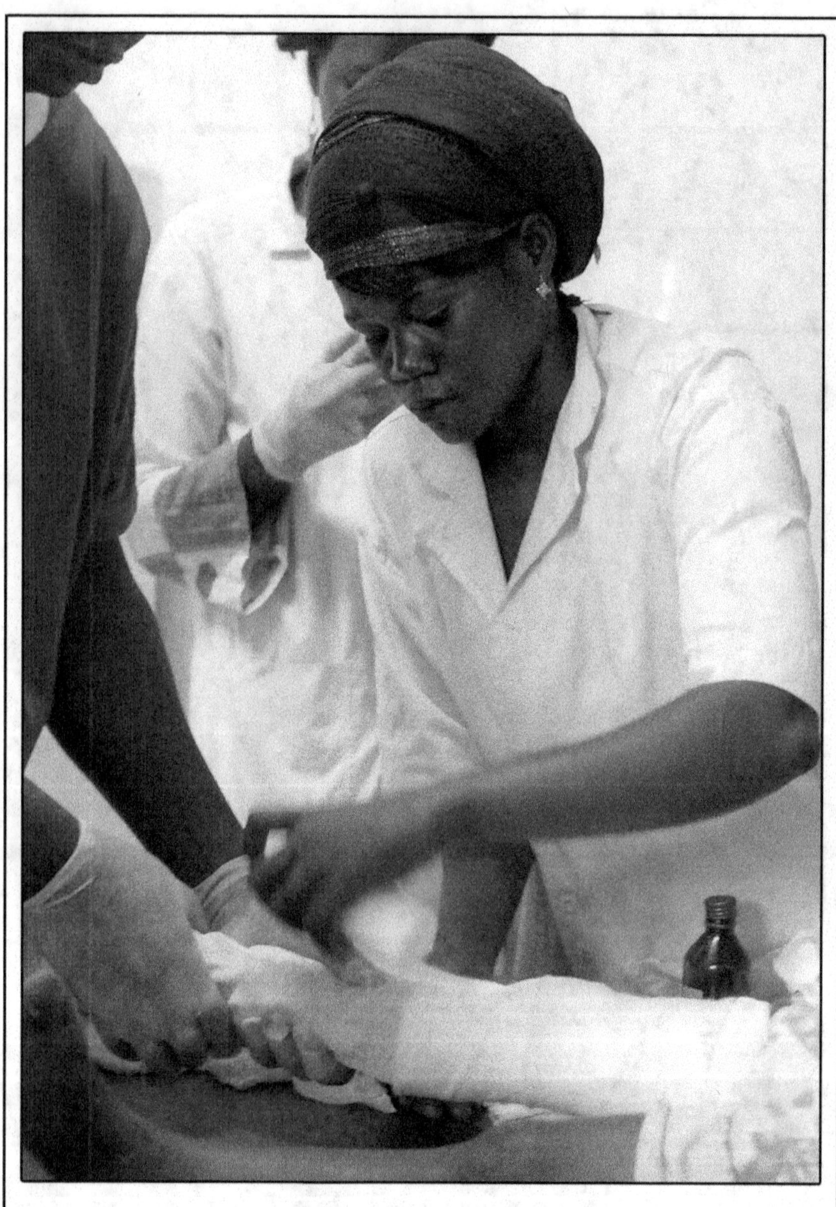

Women make up 70% of health workers
Source: World Health Organization
Photo: Andrea Merritt

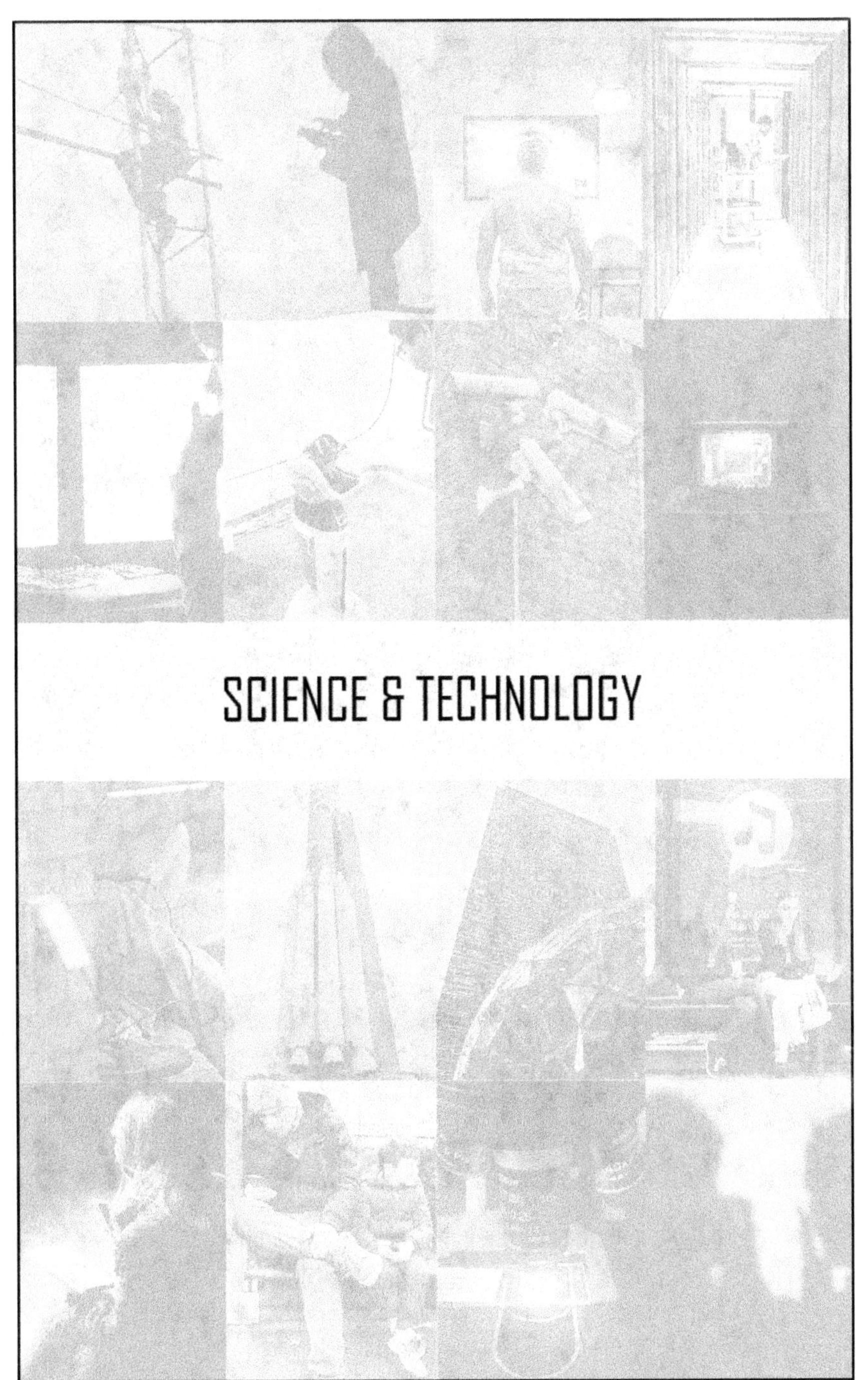

SCIENCE & TECHNOLOGY

The capacity for storing information has roughly doubled
every 40 months since the 1980s
Source: United Nations, The Sustainable Development Goals Report 2019
Photo: Jeremy Keith

90% of the data in the world
has been created in the last 2 years
Source: United Nations, The Sustainable Development Goals Report 2019
Photo: OIST

90% of the global population can access the Internet
through a 3G or higher quality network
Source:: ,International Telecommunication Union
Photo: oneVillage Initiative

At the end of 2018, 51.2% of the global population,
or 3.9 billion people, were using the Internet
Source: International Telecomunications Union
Photo: Paulo Otávio

96% of the population now lives within reach
of a mobile cellular network
Source: International Telecommunication Union
Photo: Kecko

In 2018, there were more than 5.13 billion
unique mobile users worldwide
Source: GSMA Intelligence
Photo: Kevin Dooley

More than 1.4 billion smartphones
are produced every year
Source: TrendForce
Photo: Bastian Schmidt

The proportion of women using the Internet is 12% lower
than the proportion of men using the Internet worldwide
Source: International Telecommunications Union
Photo: Derek Midgley

The proportion of young people aged 15-24 using the Internet (71%) is significantly higher than the proportion of the total population using the Internet (48%)

Source: International Telecommunication Union

Photo: John Ragai

In 104 countries,
more than 80% of the youth population are online
Source: International Telecommunication Union
Photo: Stefan Kamer

Nearly 58% of downstream traffic on the Internet is video
Source: Sandvine, Global Internet Phenomena Report
Photo: Andres Rodriguez

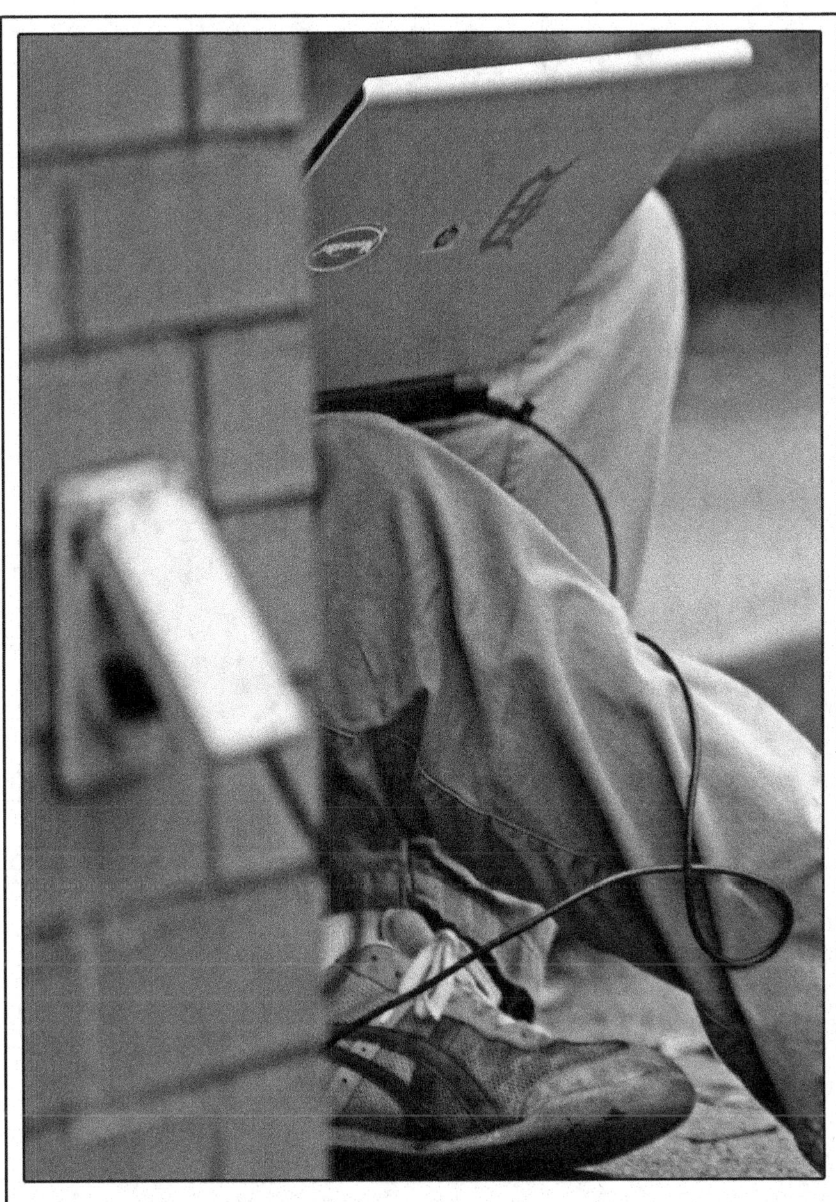

Up to 594 million people are affected by cybercrime
globally every year
Source: Center for Internet Security (CIS)
Photo: Ian Sane

The estimated annual cost to the global economy
from cybercrime is $445 billion a year
Source: McAfee & Center for Strategic and International Studies (CSIS)
Photo: Ed Ivanushkin

1/4 of the world's population
purchased goods online in 2018
Source: UNCTAD
Photo: hypothetical_E

Since the start of the century the number of couples
meeting online has more than doubled to about 1-in-5
Source: Stanford University
Photo: Kai Schreiber

There are about 2.3 billion active video gamers worldwide
Source: Computer & Communications Industry Association
Photo: Sergey Galyonkin

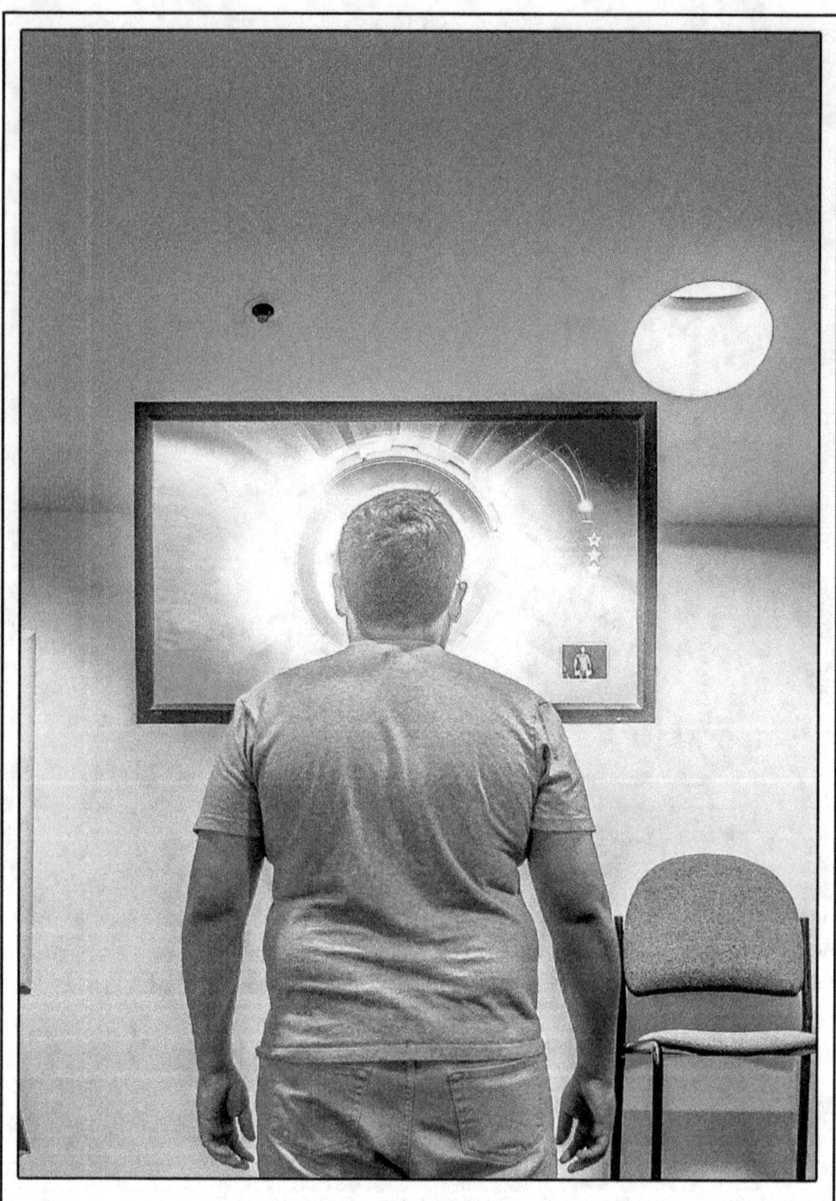

Over 850 million people watch e-sports
and other video gaming content
Source: Computer & Communications Industry Association
Photo: Sergey Galyonkin

By the end of 2018, there were an estimated 255 million users
of paid music subscription accounts globally
Source: IFPI's Global Music Report 2018
Photo: Sigfrid Lundberg

66% of people use their smartphones
to access news
Source: Digital News Report 2019
Photo: Daniel Steuri

China has been the biggest robot market in the world
since 2013
Source: International Federation of Robotics
Photo: Mitch Altman

There are more than 2000 operational satellites
currently in orbit around Earth
Source: Union of Concerned Scientists
Photo: NASA/VAFB

There were around 1.63 billion households worldwide
with televisions in 2017
Source: Digital TV Research
Photo: Rosa Menkman

Over 20% of all video surveillance cameras
are connected to the Internet
Source: IHS
Photo: Lars Plougmann

Global research and development investment reached
$2 trillion in 2016, up from $739 billion in 2000
Source: United Nations, The Sustainable Development Goals Report 2019
Photo: Magdalena Wiklund

The number of women choosing to pursue technology studies
and careers has been declining globally since the 1980s
Source: #eSkills4Girls
Photo: Barney Moss

ECONOMICS

The nominal world GDP amounted to $84.8 trillion in 2018
Source: World Bank
Photo: DocChewbacca

The top four economies combined
account for over 50% of the world economy
Source: World Economic Forum
Photo: Miguel Discart

There are over 40,000 transnational corporations
in the world
Source: Global Justice Now
Photo: Sergei F

The world's top 10 corporations have a combined revenue
of more than the 180 'poorest' countries combined
Source: Global Justice Now
Photo: Julien Chatelain

Of the 100 largest economic entities in the world,
69 are corporations and only 31 are countries
Source: Global Justice Now
Photo: Dun.can

Between 2000 and 2018, more than 790,000 merger and
acquisition transactions were announced worldwide
with a known value of over US$57 trillion
Source: Institute for Mergers, Acquisitions and Alliances
Photo: See-ming Lee

The top 1% richest individuals in the world have captured
twice as much growth as the bottom 50% since 1980
Source: Oxfam International
Photo: Daryl Mitchell

Billionaire wealth has risen by an annual average of 13% since 2010,
six times faster than the wages of ordinary workers,
which have risen by a yearly average of just 2%
Source: Oxfam International
Photo: Jim Legans, Jr

82% of all wealth created in 2017 went to the top 1%,
while the bottom 50% saw no increase at all
Source: Oxfam International
Photo: Kurtis Garbutt

Approximately 2/3 of billionaire wealth is the product of
inheritance, monopoly and cronyism
Source: Oxfam International
Photo: bradhoc

Over the next 20 years, 500 of the world's richest people
will hand over $2.4 trillion to their heirs
Source: Oxfam International
Photo: Martin Abegglen

At least 10% of the world's GDP
is deposited in offshore banks
Source: National Bureau of Economic Research
Photo: Matthew Straubmuller

An estimated \$21 to \$32 trillion of private financial wealth
is located, untaxed or lightly taxed in secrecy jurisdictions
around the world
Source: Tax Justice Network
Photo: TaxRebate.org.uk

Only 4 cents in every dollar of tax revenue
comes from taxes on wealth
Source: Oxfam International
Photo: Tim Sackton

Global annual tax losses to governments due to profit shifting
by multinational companies amount to an estimated $500 billion
Source: Tax Justice Network
Photo: Louis Bavent

More than 3.2 billion people were employed globally in 2018,
with the global unemployment rate standing at 5.38%
Source: International Labour Organization
Photo: Monika Bota

2 billion people work informally
Source: International Labour Organization
Photo: Adam Jones

93% of the world's informal employment
is in emerging and developing countries
Source: International Labour Organization
Photo: Adam Jones

While women make up less than 40% of total wage employment,
they represent 57% of part-time employees
Source: International Labour Organization
Photo: digitalpimp

There are at least 67 million domestic workers worldwide,
80% of which are women
Source: International Labour Organization
Photo: chubstock

Around 42% of workers (or 1.4 billion) worldwide
are in vulnerable forms of employment
Source: International Labour Organization
Photo: Carl Campbell

About 70% of workers do not have any insurance
to compensate them
in case of occupational diseases and injuries
Source: World Health Organization
Photo: Rod Waddington

As only 21.8% of unemployed workers
are covered by unemployment benefits,
152 million unemployed workers remain without coverage
Source: International Labour Organization
Photo: John Henderson

The youth unemployment rate (12%) is 3 times
the unemployment rate of adults (4%)
Source: International Labour Organization
Photo: Ian Livesey

Between 1999 and 2017, real wages
in developed countries increased only 9%
Source: International Labour Organization
Photo: Sascha Kohlmann

The share of national income used to remunerate workers
has shown a downward trend since 2004
Source: United Nations, The Sustainable Development Goals Report 2019
Photo: Mark McNestry

Over 80% of countries have insufficient finance
to meet national water, sanitation and hygiene targets
Source: United Nations, The Sustainable Development Goals Report 2019
Photo: Department of Foreign Affairs and Trade

More than 780 million people live
below the international poverty line of US$1.90 a day
Source: United Nations
Photo: Oskari Kettunen

26 of the world's 27 poorest countries are in Africa,
a continent that hosts more than half the world's poor
Source: World Bank
Photo: Krisztian Elek

The poorest half of the world
live on less than $5.50 a day
Source: World Bank
Photo: Bastian Greshake Tzovaras

Children make up nearly half of the almost
900 million people living on less than US$1.90 a day
Source: United Nations, The Sustainable Development Goals Report 2019
Photo: Rod Waddington

More than 200 million young people are either unemployed
or have a job but live in poverty
Source: International Labour Organization
Photo: jmettraux

80% of those who are extremely poor
live in rural areas
Source: United Nations, The Sustainable Development Goals Report 2019
Photo: Rod Waddington

2/3 of extremely poor employed workers worldwide
are agricultural workers
Source: United Nations, The Sustainable Development Goals Report 2019
Photo: Rod Waddington

8% of employed workers and their families worldwide
lived in extreme poverty in 2018
Source: United Nations, The Sustainable Development Goals Report 2019
Photo: Aravindan Ganesan

Fatal and non-fatal work-related injuries,
illness and disease cost the global economy around 4% of GDP
Source: International Labour Organization
Photo: Ian Livesey

4 billion people worldwide
are left without social protection
Source: International Labour Organization
Photo: Georg Rafisch

30% of urban residents globally have no access
to basic services or social protection
Source: UN Environment
Photo: Julien Belli

68% of people above retirement age
receive pensions
Source: United Nations, The Sustainable Development Goals Report 2019
Photo: Nicola Romagna

Only 28% of persons with severe disabilities
receive cash benefits
Source: United Nations, The Sustainable Development Goals Report 2019
Photo: Andy Isaacson (DFAT)

Only 41% of women with newborns
receive maternity benefits
Source: United Nations, The Sustainable Development Goals Report 2019
Photo: m-bot

1 out of 4 urban residents
live in slum-like conditions
Source: United Nations, The Sustainable Development Goals Report 2019
Photo: Thomas Leuthard

There are about 150 million
migrant workers around the world
Source: FAO
Photo: Lance Cheung

The industrial productivity in Europe and America
is 43 times higer than that of the least developed countries
in terms of manufacturing value added
Source: United Nations, The Sustainable Development Goals Report 2019
Photo: SBT4NOW

1% of farms in the world are larger than 50 hectares,
and they control 65% of the world's agricultural land
Source: Oxfam International
Photo: Markus Trienke

Agriculture as a whole makes up approximately 3% of global GDP
Source: World Economic Forum
Photo: Rain Moth Gallery

4 companies account for 70% of trade
in agricultural commodities globally by revenue
Source: Oxfam International
Photo: Nick Harris

Between 1971 and 2016 the global production of major food crops
– wheat, rice, maize and soy –
increased by 116%, 133%, 238% and 634% respectively
Source: Food and Agriculture Organization (FAO)
Photo: Łukasz Lech

Global annual cereal output exceeds 2.5 million tonnes
Source: FAO
Photo: Bryon Lippincott

3 conglomerates dominate nearly 60% of global turnover
for commercial seed and agricultural chemicals
Source: Oxfam International
Photo: Mike Lewinski

50 food manufacturers account for half
of all global food sales
Source: Oxfam International
Photo: Marco Verch

The global annual coffee production
is estimated at 168.77 million bags
Source: International Coffee Organization
Photo: Dennis Tang

Fisheries and aquaculture contribute about 260 million jobs
to the global economy
Source: United Nations
Photo: Aileen Devlin, Virginia Sea Grant

About 97% of the world's fishermen
live in developing countries
Source: United Nations
Photo: Benh Lieu Song

The global oceans-based economy is estimated at $3 trillion,
which is around 5% of global GDP
Source: United Nations
Photo: tetedelart1855

Shipping is responsible for more than 90%
of the trade between countries
Source: United Nations
Photo: Daniel Ramírez

Clothing production approximately doubled
during the first 15 years of the 21st century,
now exceeding 100 billion garments a year
Source: Ellen MacArthur Foundation
Photo: Sajjad Khaksari

The economic value of the global chemical industry
equates to 7.1% of the world's GDP
Source: The European Chemical Industry Council
Photo: Michael Staats

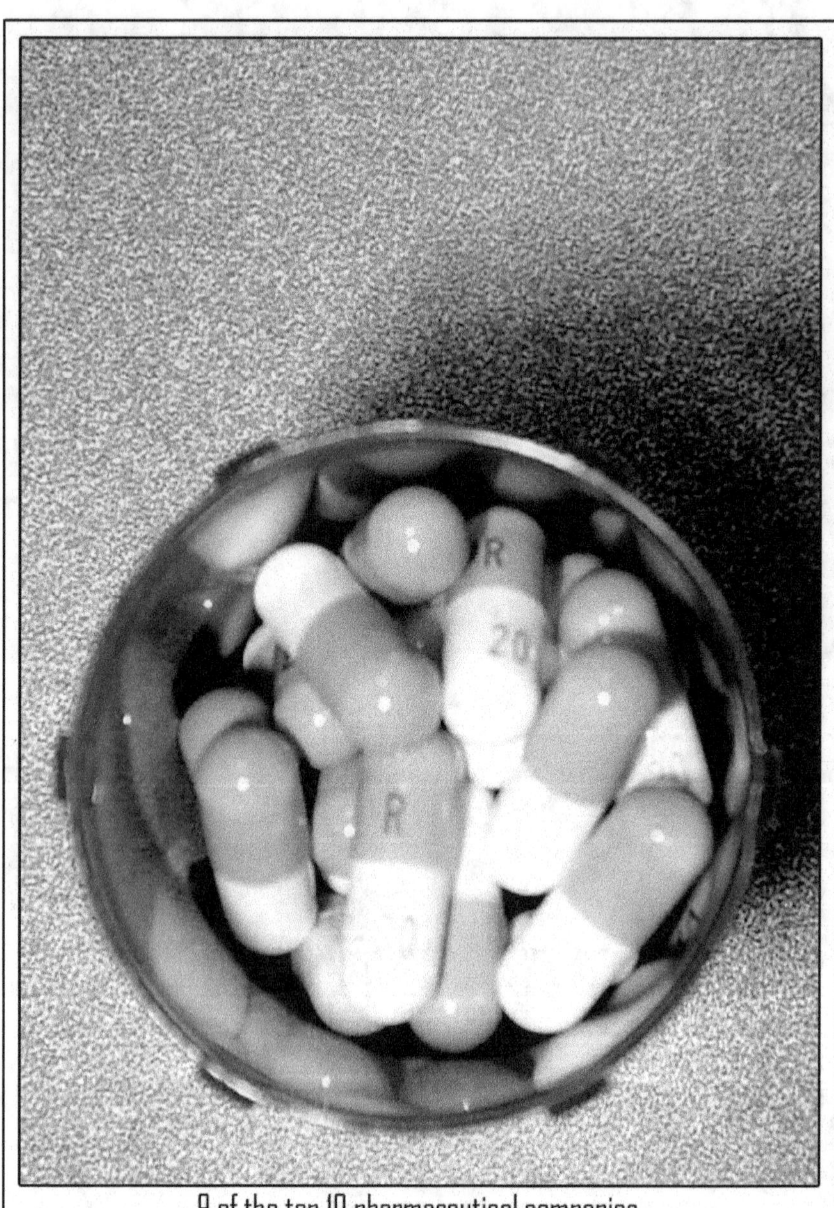

9 of the top 10 pharmaceutical companies,
the most profitable industry in the world,
spend more on marketing than on research and development
Source: Global Justice Now
Photo: BitterScripts

Advertising investment has maintained
a 0.7% share of global GDP since 2011
Source: WARC
Photo: perriscope

In 2016, influencer marketing surpassed print marketing
Source: Google Trends
Photo: Gauthier Delecroix

Consumer spending supports
approximately 60% of global GDP
Source:: ,World Economic Forum
Photo: XoMEoX

The number of payment cards
globally reached 14 billion in 2016
Source: Global Payment Cards Data and Forecasts to 2022
Photo: Ann Baekken

Some 56% of 15-year-olds in developed countries
have a bank account
Source: OECD
Photo: Timothy Neesam

The global market for waste is worth $40 billion
Source: UN Environment
Photo: Paul Morgan

The amount of research and development spent in construction
historically amounts to less than 1% of revenues
Source: Medium
Photo: Finn Terman Frederiksen

Productivity in the construction industry has grown
at just 1% annually for the past 20 years
Source: BCC Research
Photo: AJ Oswald

Real estate money laundering schemes are estimated
to reach $1.6 trillion a year worldwide
Source: Accuity
Photo: Paul Sableman

Consumers spend about $871 billion,
or roughly 1% of the global GDP, on air travel
Source: International Air Transport Association (IATA)
Photo: Chris Sampson

International tourist arrivals rose from 25 million in 1950
to more than 1.2 billion in 2016, a 49-fold increase
Source: United Nations World Tourism Organization
Photo: Pablo Castro

Travel & Tourism generated 10.4%
of all global economic activity in 2018
Source: WTTC
Photo: Richie Diesterheft

319 million jobs were linked to
the global tourism sector in 2018
Source: WTTC
Photo: Floris Oosterveld

Finished automobiles are the top good traded worldwide
with $1.35 trillion being traded each year between countries
Source: Business Insider
Photo: Phil Richards

Total global military spending
is now 76% higher than the post-cold war low in 1998
Source: Stockholm International Peace Research Institute
Photo: Expert Infantry

The global theatrical and home entertainment market
generated $96.8 billion in 2018
Source: Motion Picture Association of America
Photo: Jakob Montrasio

Around 1.7 million jobs have already been lost
to robots globally since 2000
Source: Financial Post
Photo: South African Tourism

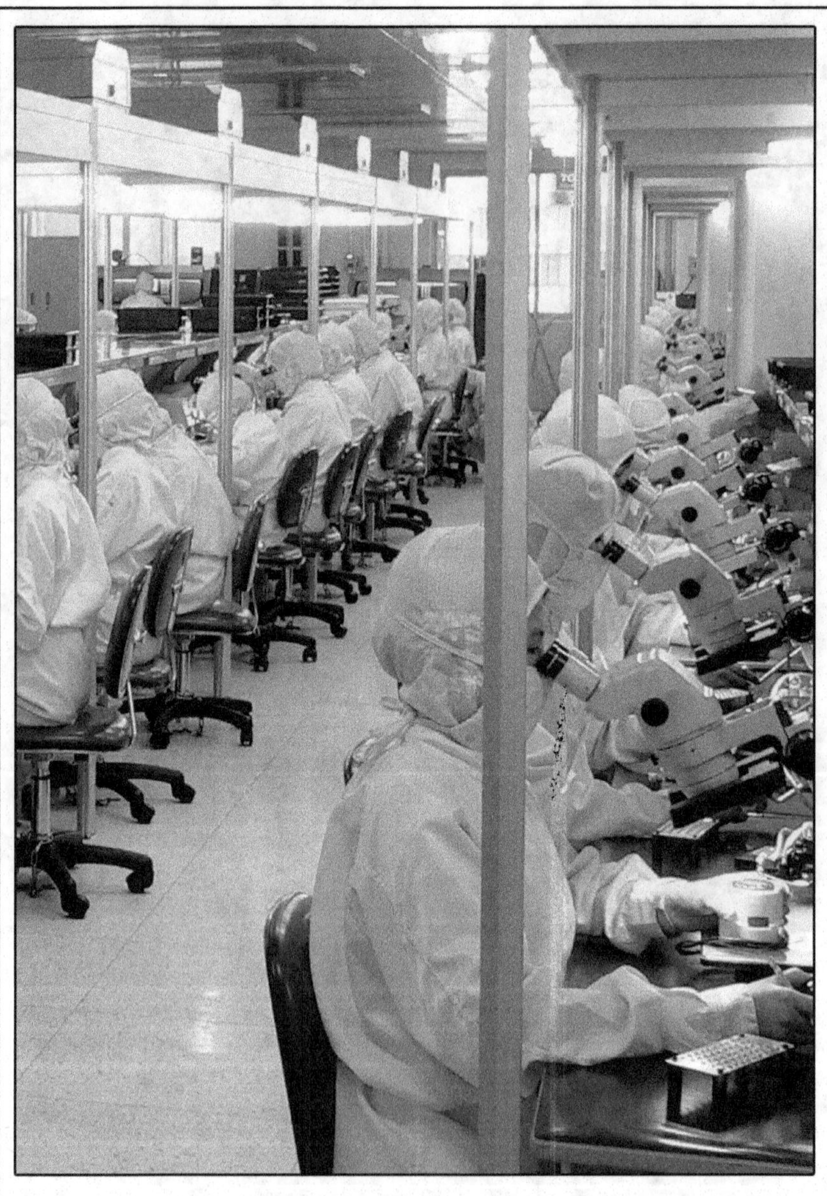

About 50% of current jobs globally could be automated
Source: McKinsey Global Institute
Photo: Steve Jurvetson

Google holds a 92.74%
search engine market share worldwide
Source: StatCounter
Photo: F. Delventhal

Cooperatives provide at least 279 million jobs
Source: International Labour Organization
Photo: Tim Green

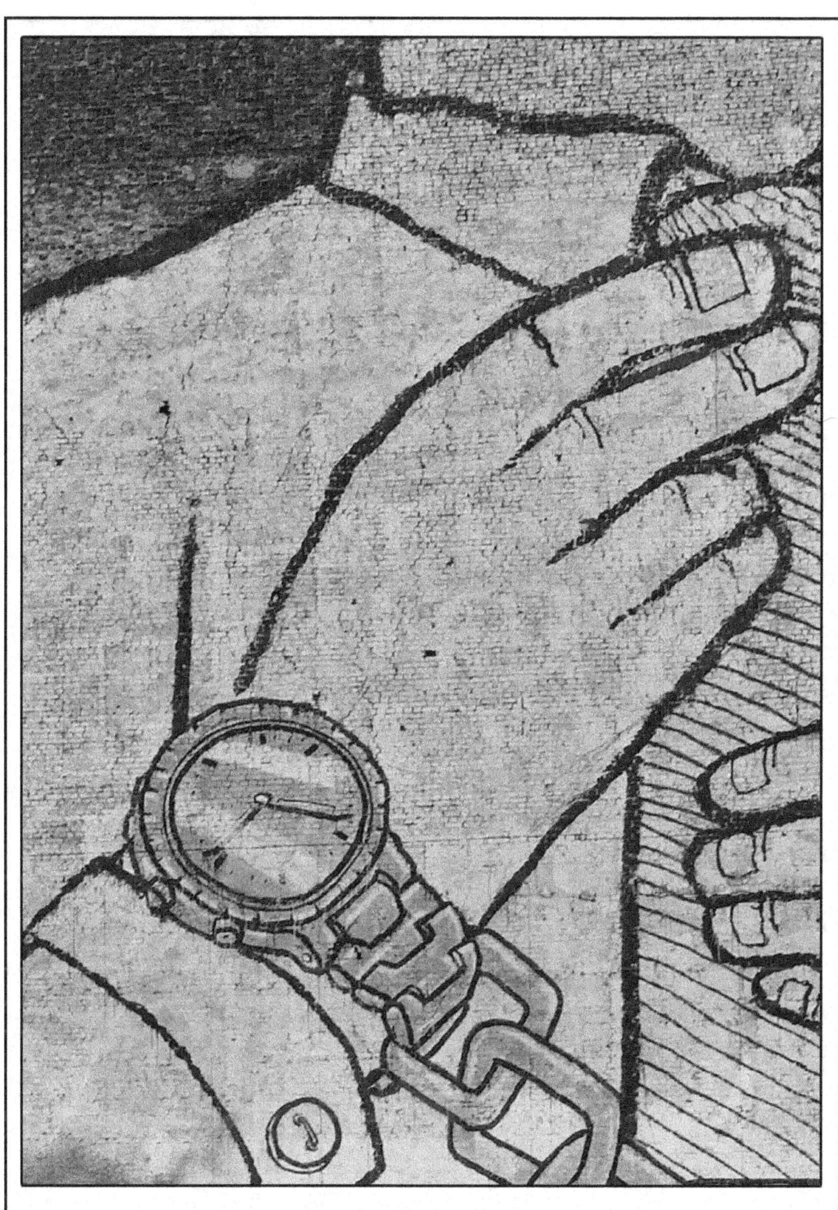

9 out of 10 billionaires are men
Source: Forbes The World's Billionaires 2017 Ranking
Photo: Emanuele

13% of the global population
still lacks access to modern electricity
Source: United Nations, The Sustainable Development Goals Report 2019
Photo: damn unique

On average, the world's debt exceeds $86,000 in per capita terms, which is more than 2½ times the average income per-capita
Source: International Monetary Fund
Photo: Jeremy Bronson

Worldwide, the private sector's debt
has tripled since 1950
Source: International Monetary Fund
Photo: Michael Swan

Nature provides services worth around
US$125 trillion a year
Source:: WWF, Living Planet Report 2018
Photo: Beyond Coal & Gas Image Library

In 2017, Wall Street bonuses went back to pre-crisis levels,
reaching an average of $184,220, the highest since 2006
Source: New York State Comptroller
Photo: Edgar Jiménez